Badgers at my Window

I grew up on the edge of the industrial Black Country, where my father was a doctor, and have been determined to be a naturalist as long as I can remember.

I caught newts and caterpillars, as a child. I went ferreting and birdsnesting, as a boy; and I struck up friendships with gamekeepers and poachers and rat catchers, who were patients of my father. They may have lacked formal scientific education, but they taught me more practical natural history than all my school-masters.

Ten years constant companionship with a tame badger that I had handreared put the final seal on my longing to settle in quiet places among the wildlife I love. So I broke free from a secure job in industry fifteen years ago to earn a more precarious living by writing and broad-casting about my work.

Of the fourteen books now published under my name, all but three have natural history themes. I broadcast on similar subjects and my greatest reward is the friendship of folk with similar tastes whom I should not otherwise have met.

I am equally happy arguing (or agreeing) with them or spending long, lonely hours, sharing my wood with the creatures which live there.

PHIL DRABBLE

Badgers at my Window

Phil Drabble

Illustrated by Stanley Porter <small>FRPS</small>

FONTANA/COLLINS

To Jess
For sharing the joys
our badgers bestow

First published in Great Britain by Pelham Books Ltd 1969
First issued in Fontana 1976

Copyright © Phil Drabble 1969

Made and printed in Great Britain by
William Collins Sons & Co. Ltd, Glasgow

CONDITIONS OF SALE: This book is sold subject to the
condition that it shall not, by way of trade or otherwise,
be lent, re-sold, hired out or otherwise circulated without
the publisher's prior consent in any form of binding or
cover other than that in which it is published and without
a similar condition including this condition being imposed
on the subsequent purchaser

Contents

Illustrations

All photographs by Stanley Porter FRPS

Preface

The accepted English word for persistent persecution is 'Badgered' because so many generations have treated this most delightful animal so foully.

Baiting, with dogs, in organized badger pits has long-since been illegal but it was only in 1973 that the Badger Act was passed to outlaw the 'sport' of badger digging and to prevent the ignorant cruelty of those who snared and gassed them.

It is now illegal to keep captive badgers as pets, so that it would be illegal to hand rear the badgers described in this book without a licence from the Nature Conservancy.

Unfortunately, this encouraging legislation lacks teeth to enforce it. It is only illegal to kill badgers 'wilfully', as I found to my disgust when I found a dead badger in a snare and asked the police to make a prosecution.

All that was needed for successful defence was to claim that the snare had been legally set to catch a fox and that the badger had been caught accidentally!

I am on the badger's side, not because I am a sentimentalist, but because I have found by experience that badgers are grossly maligned.

I am lucky enough to live among them and enjoy their company and I hope that, when readers have shared the experience with me, there will be a few less in the world who will try to call down doom on the badgers' heads.

P. D.

Foreword

BY BRIAN VESEY-FITZGERALD

Some thirty years ago, when I was Editor-in-Chief of
The Field, an article arrived on my desk – and I should
stress that I used to get a great many such unsolicited
articles every day – from Phil Drabble. It was obvious
that the author was young and enthusiastic: it was also
obvious that his article was quite unsuitable. (I have since
learnt that it was the first that he had ever written!)
But there was something about that article which
prompted me not to use the usual rejection slip, but to
ask him to write another article on some subject with
which he was really familiar. He did and I published it.
And I am very proud indeed to have been the first person
to publish Phil Drabble.

He belongs to the old school of sportsman-naturalist:
a school which is now, more's the pity, virtually extinct.
He is a countryman with the countryman's unsentimental
knowledge of and regard for animals; and his knowledge
of the wild animals of our countryside is immense.

But there is something more, an indefinable something
which might perhaps best be described as a 'genius for
contact' with animals. He has tamed a wide variety of
wild animals. 'Tamed' is not really the right word, for
taming implies subjugation. The old-fashioned 'gentled'
would be the correct term, for Phil and his animals live
on equal terms. I have myself seen stoat and weasel in
the Drabble household. Had I not seen the stoat I would
never have believed it possible. And the badger of
Chapter Two did once deign to notice me, squatting

momentarily on my shoe.

But do not make the mistake of thinking that this is just a book about tame, about gentled, badgers. It is not. I have learnt more about badgers – and I have myself been closely interested in them for more than half a century – from this book than from all the books and all the scientific papers that have come my way: and been given more food for thought. And I feel sure that that will be equally true for every reader.

And I feel sure about something else: that this book is destined to become a classic.

CHAPTER ONE

Background

The window, within a yard of my study desk, is smeared with thick, glutinous clay from the wood outside.

Although the sliding panes shut snug enough to exclude any draught which is perceptible to my blunt human senses, it is obvious that a powerful human pong seeps out.

Every night a boar badger appears at the mouth of his sett under the hawthorn tree and settles down to a meditative scratch. He uses his latrine pit and then ambles off into the night.

He doesn't go to the wood, to forage, nor to the pool, to drink. His first call is to my study window, which he tests for any tell-tale draughts for clues that one or other sliding pane is not securely shut. You can see him – on a daylight visit – in illustration 14 of this book.

If he is lucky and there is the slightest crack, he hooks his powerful claw round the edge of the glass and heaves. Each pane weighs more than a hundredweight and needs a considerable effort to overcome its initial inertia and start it sliding freely. But the badger's strength is so prodigious that he can flick it open with an effortless shrug of his great shoulder.

Once inside, he tries the door and, if he is lucky again, he has the freedom of the house and wanders round until he comes to us.

He is not often lucky though. Unsupervised, adult boar badgers find upholstered furniture irresistible. The least creak of a spring is all the excuse they need to rip open the cover and investigate the noise. So we are careful to leave the window fastened tight.

He takes this as a personal insult, sniffs the edge of the panes and attacks them with the energy he would need to excavate a sett in solid rock, plastering the un-resisting glass with mud in reward for its obduracy.

Soon he is joined by two sow badgers, who are less interested in burglary, so he gives up the unequal struggle and wanders off with them to forage in the wood.

This experiment in 'keeping' tame badgers at complete liberty is the culmination of ambitions which were born in boyhood days.

The initial spark of my interest was kindled in my mind by *The Wind In The Willows*. It was read aloud to me, long before I could decipher the written word for myself, and my favourite character was Mr Brock, the badger.

Soon I was reading everything I could lay my hands on, which was even remotely concerned with badgers, swallowing tales of the crimes they committed, the sport they gave and the good they did with impartial rapacity.

It so happened that one of the first books I stumbled on gave a vivid account of what must surely have been one of the most breakneck sports devised by Man.

Proceedings were started by leaving a boy, at sunset, to watch a badger sett. He was given the strictest instructions not to move a muscle until the badgers had emerged and disappeared for at least half an hour.

Then, he was to report to the sportsmen, who had sensibly retired to the comfort and hospitality of the nearest local inn.

All but one continued their convivial task, while the odd man out crept up to the deserted sett and pegged an open-mouthed sack, very firmly, at the entrance to each hole. Then he returned for his friends and their dogs.

The dogs could be almost any breed, because, once entered to badgers, most dogs are keen to hunt them. A foxhound or two, which had grown too old for conventional packs, were ideal and gave the whole thing an air of some respectability.

It was essential to choose a bright, moonlight night and desirable, I imagine, to have been at the 'local' long enough to have imbibed a bellyful of Dutch courage.

The badgers, meanwhile, had had time to wander a mile or so from home and, when all was ready, the 'hounds' were laid on the trail, which started at their sett.

At first, the line was old and cold, so that even the hounds with delicate noses would have difficulty in owning it. It gave the followers the chance to accustom their eyes to the gloom before they had to rush, buck's neck, over almost impossible terrain.

Gradually the scent warmed up and the still night air resounded to the mournful tongues of hunting hounds.

Once the badgers were alerted, they made for home, leaving the hounds to puzzle out the aimless maze of their wanderings after food. It must have been a sport which laid heavy odds against the hunters.

If hounds were laid on too soon after the badgers left their sett, they would have nothing better than a scamper round the wood. If the badgers had too much start, or scent was poor, they would get home too far ahead and would have plenty of time to scratch a way into the sett, without getting involved with the sacks left there to trap them.

Ideally, hounds should be so close on their quarry's tail that he had to make a headlong dash to escape, which would bundle him right into the bag.

Even then, the followers had to be close enough to heave bag and badger out before he had time to rip his way to freedom.

I have no idea how widespread such moonlight madness was, but the account of it so inflamed my imagination that for years I yearned to try it.

I never got the chance and, now, it is too late because my affection for badgers has grown so deep that, far from harassing them, I am always ready to leap to their defence.

I have become, instead, more and more obsessed with an unquenchable desire to learn more and more about their habits and their loves and their hates.

One of the penalties of acquiring such a reputation for being fond of badgers – as opposed to being fond of hunting them! – is that it becomes impossible to remain unaware how dreadfully they are persecuted.

This may not be a bad thing because, however unpleasant it is, it does at least hone an edge on one's determination to procure legal protection for them.

In spring, I am frequently asked how to rear young badger cubs as pets. By then it is usually too late to explain that I have learned, by bitter experience, that badgers are completely unfitted for captivity, and how difficult it is to return them to the wild, when once they have tasted life behind bars.

In summer it is all too common to hear of badgers pining their hearts out in little zoos of ill repute. Few animals make less satisfactory exhibits because they spend their days curled motionless as hedgehogs in a corner. By night they shatter teeth and nails in frustrated struggles to escape.

If they are supplied with straw, they bury themselves, so that there is nothing to see but a pile of straw. They scratch and bite at wooden kennels, so that it is obviously inevitable that they will tear themselves free, and it is all too common to see them in concrete runs and cold iron dens.

No animal loves his creature comforts more nor snuggles down with greater delight into the warm luxury of soft bedding.

Yet it is useless to report these unkempt zoo badgers to the RSPCA because our protective laws are so sloppy that nothing can be done without proof of positive cruelty.

By autumn the season's crop of hand-reared badgers is growing up. Many people buy a cub in spring with high hopes, the best intentions and no imagination.

For a few weeks it is a tremendous thrill to bottle rear it and to watch it growing from a cuddly toy to a playful cub. But few people have the time to give the necessary attention with unfailing regularity.

Holidays and week-ends and invitations to parties intervene.

The daily chore of mucking out pens begins to lose its glamour, expenses mount beyond expectations and gently playful cubs grow rough and boisterous.

Once the cub is weaned, the temptation is to put a bowl of food into the run each evening and leave handling and showing affection to him till there is more time at week-ends.

Badgers are exceptionally companionable and demonstrative creatures with limitless energy.

Solitary confinement first makes them pine and eventually sours their tempers.

When week-ends come, they are so overjoyed at human approach that they cram eight days of energy into eight minutes' play. An over-exuberant cub, by autumn, is strong enough and rough enough to draw blood from flaccid human hands with sheer *joie de vivre*.

This is when people who have heard how fond I am of badgers ring me up about their cubs.

'We reared a cub, in spring,' they say, 'but he has grown unaccountably savage.' Or 'We are going on our holiday and want to get rid of our cub. The local zoos won't have him, so we're thinking of setting him free. Where do you suggest?'

Or, worse still, 'We think the world of our young badger, but can't keep him any longer. Would you like him?'

I can see precisely what the problem is, from their viewpoint. Unfortunately I know the problem from the badger's side as well.

It is extremely cruel to turn tame young badgers loose. They won't be able to fend for themselves and, having lost their fear of Man, they may avoid starvation by attacking his poultry.

This will not only bring down swift retribution on their heads, but it gets badgers, in general, an undeserved bad name.

If a liberated cub does survive human persecution and learns to fend for itself, it is almost certain to fall victim to attacks by its own kind, as I was to discover later.

With zoos and freedom out of the question, pressure, to persuade me to take it on, naturally mounts and, if I had no badgers of my own, the temptation would be irresistible.

As things are, the kindest advice I can give is to destroy unwanted cubs and to be strong-willed enough never to accept one again.

Winter brings badger digging and pleas to exert what influence I have to get it banned.

I am not anti-sporting and believe that it is no business of mine to question *why* people enjoy hunting or shooting or fishing.

The important thing to me is not why they hunt, but what quarry they choose and how they kill it.

On this basis, I would do all in my power to obtain for otters the same total protection that the law accords to rare birds.

This is partly because poisonous pesticides, unavoidable mounting human pressure on the countryside and changing fashions of agriculture have put the survival of otters into serious jeopardy.

The added – and unnecessary – hazard from huntsmen could be the last straw.

My antipathy to otter hunting is not confined to adding to the perils of a species already finding it hard to survive. I hate the methods used as well. It is not my idea of 'sporting' to line river banks with hunt followers, whose banshee yells tell hounds where their quarry is, every time he comes to the surface for air.

Without this unfair aid of spectators scanning the water, the hounds and huntsman alone would kill few otters.

Foxes, on the other hand, are in no danger of extinction, and anyone who has seen a tortured fox, waiting for merciful release from the wire snare, which half strangles him, might well think swift death by hounds no worse.

Badgers fall somewhere between the two. They have increased in numbers since the last war and are probably in less peril from Man now than at any time in the last two hundred years.

Public opinion has become more enlightened, and more people appreciate how little harm most badgers do, and how much good.

The Forestry Commission is a good example of this. Until recently, badgers were destroyed in or near plantations because they forced their way under wire netting, leaving gaps for the rabbits to enter and destroy the young trees.

It has now been realized what a boon badgers are, because they kill so many voles and insect pests, the Commission give them full protection and put swinging badger doors in their netting, which allow them to pass through but keep the rabbits out.

There is no need, at the moment, to control badger numbers because they are not so common that their normal food supply is not sufficient.

Badger digging, in any case, is an ineffective method of doing so, and had no merit as sport. The dig begins by putting a terrier into one of the tunnel entrances of the sett, where he soon disappears from sight.

He searches below ground until he comes to the cavity, or 'overn', which the badgers have hollowed out to be their bed.

The thrilling scent here excites him to throw his tongue and his chorus of hate can be heard from above, giving the signal for the diggers to work feverishly and dig down to the spot where their quarry is kennelled.

So far there has been no cruelty. The badger's slumbers have merely been troubled by a rude little dog, yelling noisy abuse from a safe distance of two or three feet.

A badger will sometimes charge his foe and the purpose of breeding working terriers small and low to ground is to allow them to move freely in a nine-inch tunnel, and to dodge the punishment a larger dog would be unable to avoid.

But working terriers are often psychologically as bumptious as little men. The ones which are foolhardy enough to allow the badger to get to grips with them will get the worst end of the stick. It is the one sport which is more cruel to the hunter than the hunted.

This makes it no more desirable. As the diggers get closer and closer, the dog, emboldened by the illusion that help, which is so close, is bound to be effective, sometimes mixes it with his adversary and is terribly mauled for his pains.

In theory, the only time he should attack is when the badger turns to dig himself further in. A bold terrier should then force his quarry to turn in self defence. If he does not, the badger can often dig himself in faster than men with spades can tunnel down to him.

When the diggers eventually do reach their dog, they pull him out by his tail and that is the reason why a terrier's tail is docked to just a hand's breadth.

Only when the dog has been pulled out does the real cruelty begin. The badger, which is then exposed to view, is often extracted with steel badger tongs. These diabolical instruments of torture are long-handled steel tongs, similar to the tools blacksmiths use to handle red-hot iron for forging.

The animal is gripped by these, usually by one of his legs, and the pressure that unimaginative morons apply, aided by the leverage of those long handles, can easily be imagined.

What happens next does not bear thinking about, especially if a dog has been stupid enough to get mauled and a 'fond' owner wants to get his revenge.

In any case, relatively few badgers are caught by

digging because the sheer hard labour involved limits the number of people who cannot find a more congenial pastime.

So digging is not worth serious consideration as a method of control (even supposing control was necessary); and as a 'sport', even when properly conducted, the temptation to inflict torment on the badger, as a reward for catching him, is often more than the type of people who indulge in it can resist.

The fact that I am known to be extremely fond of badgers results in an annual flood of evidence about the malpractices of digging, in the hope that I shall be able to do something about it.

Perhaps this book may prove to be some contribution towards the badger's cause.

Those who regard badgers as 'sporting' quarry, to test the mettle of their dogs, are not their only enemy.

Old-fashioned gamekeepers hate them too. Indeed, old-fashioned gamekeepers frequently hate all predators and are utterly impervious to any argument that a bird with a hooked bill or an animal with canine teeth can have any good in it at all.

No arguments about rarity or the balance of harm and good are tolerated. Last year I met a man who was prepared to slaughter a rare pine marten, which he thought had killed half a dozen pheasants, although there are literally thousands of pheasants to every marten.

He was interested in pheasants for sport and was prepared to exterminate anything which killed one or even competed with them for food. It turned out that the killer was a colony of rats, which is some measure of his ignorance.

Rats probably do more harm to shooting men than all of the creatures they class as vermin, but barn owls, which prey on young rats, are just as likely to get a charge of lead shot as a carrion crow.

I am convinced that weasels do the game preserver more good than harm, and, in any case, there is surely room in the countryside for creatures other than pheasants and partridges.

Those who preach the dogma of *total* preservation of all species do their cause more harm than good, because uncontrolled vandals, in the wild, will thrive at the expense of inoffensive neighbours, just as they do in our society.

The practical approach is to conserve a sensible balance, by a constructive wildlife management policy, which maintains a deliberate balance between hunters and hunted.

There is no such thing as a natural balance of Nature because the conditions which control population increase or decrease are always changing. If everything is left to itself, anarchy prevails and the strong inevitably prosper at the expense of the weak.

Naturalists have no monopoly of this knowledge and I know many first-rate keepers who actively encourage a population of predators to cull out wild weaklings and arrest the spread of disease.

But, where there is a bad keeper, badgers need no other enemy. The most cursory examination of a badger sett discloses whether it is occupied – and a dose of cyanide gas ensures that they never emerge.

It is of course illegal to gas badgers, but trespassers are so few on well-keepered estates that gas attacks are almost impossible to detect or to prove.

Old-fashioned steel gins are patient custodians of secret places, and what the eye doesn't see will cause no grief. Gins, too, are illegal in England and Wales, though

Scotland is not yet so civilized.

The wrong sort of keepers do not even confine themselves to killing badgers from the land they control.

Badgers wander over a wide territory and sometimes visit other colonies a mile or so from 'home'. They travel by traditional routes and the tracks their regular journeys leave in the undergrowth, or through gaps in hedges, are padded hard and clear for observant eyes to see.

A wire noose, cleverly set, does not only hang the current crop. The tracks used by succeeding generations are as traditional as the setts. A determined man, by regularly gassing one sett, can wreak havoc over a wide area because the badgers from other setts will flow in to fill a vacant area as surely as water will find its own level.

The flood of facts in Natural History programmes, on wireless and television, newspaper articles and scientific research, backed by the increasing weight of public opinion, is gradually converting the more intelligent shooting men and their keepers.

Combined with the changing policy of the Forestry Commission, this is providing large areas where badgers can thrive more or less unmolested, so that their population shows signs of increasing, at least locally.

The snag is that there are also places where badgers simply cannot be allowed to thrive, and these exceptions can always be produced as an unanswerable argument against those who advocate a policy of *total* protection.

It is the old argument between preservation and conservation. I would prefer to see a law passed to prohibit destruction of badgers *except* by specific licence, possibly issued by the Nature Conservancy but definitely not by the Ministry of Agriculture, who have forfeited any claim to respect in my mind by their weakness in issuing licences to lay narcotic baits for woodpigeons.

This has been an example of political double-talk which has plumbed the lowest depths. 'Narcotics,' they say, 'are not poisons, they are just drugs.' They cannot deny, however, that creatures taking an overdose will not recover. There is nothing they can do to prevent other birds, or animals, than woodpigeons taking their bait, so that, however they phrase it, they are really giving a licence for the indiscriminate laying of poison bait.

Nevertheless, I believe that there should be the possibility of getting a licence to remove badgers from the places where they may literally endanger life or do serious damage to crops.

It is easy enough to prove that they do little or no harm in woodland and that, on balance, they are likely to be a positive asset. But a sett on farmland can be a serious hazard.

There is a bank on my neighbour's farm, for example, which falls away steeply to a deep ditch. The soil is well drained and warm, providing an ideal site.

Tunnels have been driven horizontally, from the hedge-bank side, twenty or thirty yards under the surface of the field.

When the land was used for grazing, no great damage was done, because any holes that did break surface were simply used as additional exits or entrances.

But when the time came to plough the field, the heavy tractor crowned in the crust over the first deep tunnel and lurched to a halt at a dangerous angle. It was like driving a car across an open man-hole.

Naturally the farmer wanted the hazard removing before harvest, when there would be the additional weight of a giant combine and heavy trailer of grain.

Many people would simply have gassed the colony and said nothing about it.

Certainly, if there was a law to give complete protection, most people would simply take the law into their own hands.

In this case, I was called in for advice. It was perfectly plain that something had got to be done, and something fairly drastic. So I offered to empty the sett – and keep it empty.

Instead of using gas, I used Reynardine, which is a liquid sold by agricultural chemists to deter unwanted animals. It has a very powerful smell, like strong creosote, and though extremely persistent is not poisonous. Balls of string can be soaked in it and stretched round plants, to keep rabbits off, and it can be put down rabbit holes, to make them lie out, or be used to discourage deer.

I soaked a bucketful of sawdust in the stuff, and put a trowelful in each hole in the sett, filling the mouths of the holes with earth, as I went along, to prevent the stink dispersing on the wind. Next day, one hole had been opened up by the badgers, who had evidently decided to move to pleasanter quarters. I filled that up again, to delay their return as long as possible.

The operation was entirely successful, but only temporary. In about two months the badgers were back and I had to repeat the operation.

Now that I have been working on the sett for some time, one dose lasts about three months, but it is absolutely vital to make certain the sett is completely deserted before the breeding season in February.

When there are cubs in the sett, too young for the sow to move, she will tolerate almost anything rather than be parted from them. It would obviously be grossly unfair to put such pressure on her that she was forced to leave her young to perish, and the only alternative is to oust her before she has them.

I happen to be enthusiastic enough to take on this chore rather than see a colony destroyed. It might be impractical to expect a farmer, with no strong feelings either way, to go to the same trouble.

So it seems sensible to allow the odd colony, which can be proved to be such a hazard, to be humanely destroyed by a pest officer, with a Nature Conservancy licence granted for that specific sett.

A more sweeping law, which couldn't be enforced, would simply let in the local badger digging club or the local hunt.

Hunting men want foxes above ground, where their hounds can hunt them. Common practice is to send a terrier man round, the night before they meet, with instructions to block all earths, while the foxes are out for the night.

Next morning – in theory – they find the earth stopped, when they return, lie out in thick cover above ground, and are forced to give a long run for the simple reason that their normal havens of escape are stopped up.

In practice, if there are badgers sharing the earths, the plan may flop. Badgers do not normally relish spending the day above ground and are not easily deterred by earth stoppers.

If they come home to find the front door locked, their remedy is simple. They set-to with powerful claws to clear the obstruction or dig a new way in, and the fringe benefit to the fox is he then has a ready-made way of escape.

It is a small crime for which to forfeit a life, but I

once watched the Hunt open up an artificial earth till they got down to the badger, which they forced to run for it.

The hounds closed in, but the badger was too tough and, when a few hounds had been well and truly lamed, the bulk of the pack stood back and roared encouragement to the few 'bold' ones, which made dashing attacks from the rear, retreating when he turned.

Eventually, a hunt servant put him out of his misery with a humane killer.

I told the woman who owned the cover what I thought about her but I was assured that the badger had bolted, and not been turned down to hounds, so there was nothing illegal about it and no satisfactory action I could take.

It is something which does not often happen because most hunts are not stupid enough to flout public opinion to that extent. Besides which, the risk to hounds' feet, if they mix it with a badger, is just not worth it. So they often encourage the local badger diggers to do the job quietly instead.

Badgers can be killed by ignorant kindness too. Opponents of hunting frequently complain that foxes are bred for sport, in the same way that pheasants are.

The fact is that hunting men build artificial earths, consisting of a subterranean brick chamber or 'kennel', like a man-hole for a drain, with two tunnels leading into it. These are normally drainpipes of nine inches diameter, each about ten yards long.

These artificial earths are built in quiet, secluded places in woodland or odd corners of derelict land on farms.

Foxes are not bred in them artificially, in the sense that pheasants are reared and put into covert, but, if the earths are cleverly constructed and sited, they adopt them as breeding quarters from choice, as tits take over artificial nesting boxes.

Hunting men then know where to find their foxes, or where they will try to escape when put out of kale or other cover, as surely as naturalists know the territory which birds will choose with the aid improvements to their natural habitat.

It is, of course, a form of preservation which anti-hunting folk deplore because they say that foxes could easily be controlled by other means than hunting. They are not always angered so much by the intrinsic cruelty of hunting as by the fact that hunting men enjoy it.

An alternative that they advocate is to gas the earths between the months of March and May.

In theory, the vixens will still be lying up with their cubs at this time of year so that both mother and young will be poisoned together.

In practice, there is no means of knowing if it is a fox or badger which lies hidden underground. Badgers will take to artificial earths, or 'drains', as readily as foxes, and foxes often share naturally-dug badger setts with their rightful owners.

The result of gassing may be that the badgers are sacrificed, not to make death easier for foxes or to control their numbers, but to ensure that men cannot be 'degraded' by the enjoyment of their hunting instinct.

If this practice is made respectable in law (it is illegal to gas badgers now) keepers with old-fashioned ideas would gas *all* earths, in case they contained a fox. They would do this even if the evidence pointed quite clearly to badgers as the tenants.

I would much prefer the law to ban the use of gas entirely except by trained, professional pest officers, who would shoulder the responsibility of ensuring that they gassed nothing by accident.

They would be prohibited from gassing any earth which might contain a badger, except by special licence, and would keep a comprehensive register of every earth they gassed.

Then, if there was any suspicion that powers were being misused, the earth in question could be opened up and evidence obtained to show the species and cause of death of any victims buried there.

However sparingly powers are used, it does seem essential to provide legislation capable of dealing with the odd 'rogue' badgers and those which take up residence on agricultural land, where heavy machinery is used, or other places where it is not sensible to allow them.

It is just as unreasonable for protectionists to demand total protection, in all circumstances, as it is for game preservers and sportsmen to wipe out every badger they can lay their hands on.

CHAPTER TWO

Bloody Bill Brock

Henry Williamson's story about Bloody Bill Brock set the seal on my interest which had started with *The Wind In The Willows*.

I read the story again and again, thrilled by the natural history and enthralled by the descriptions of badger digging, which are vivid as a horror film.

Although it is our largest mammal, except for seals and deer, very little has been written about the badger and surprisingly few hard facts are known about it. So I decided to collect what factual evidence I could for myself.

I had been badger digging and been sickened, first by the punishment the terriers suffered at the jaws of the badger and then by what happened to the badger at the hands of men.

I had spent what time I could, watching wild badgers at their sett, which had taught me something of the limitations of such vigils.

The nearest sett to me was four miles away and, for a good part of the year, I did not get home till after dusk, when it would have been too dark to watch whatever activity did take place.

Summer months were grand, because the cubs were active and had not yet learned the meaning of caution. They give an entirely misleading picture of life because, if the adults were not more stealthy and secretive the race would long since have been extinct.

Even so, it is possible to learn a great deal about play

and grooming and sanitation and the time they first appear at night, even by watching cubs.

By the time they are ready to go off to forage, the delight is still there, but it is far more difficult to observe what it is that they are doing.

Within a few minutes of showing up, they melt into the surrounding shadows to feed and it is difficult to watch what they eat or where or how they find it.

We used to spend a good deal of our holidays at a fishing hotel, remote in Central Wales, though it was not the fishing which attracted us.

We liked the company there, because no one would have gone who was not fond of country things. And, because of the seclusion, the mixture of wild hills and woods and the river at the bottom of the lawn, the wealth of bird life was superb.

Buzzards nested in the oaks above the hotel, there were pied flycatchers and goldcrests and dippers and curlew and stonechats and wheatears.

When we first went, there were red squirrels in the stately trees in the garden but now they have been replaced by their cousins the ubiquitous greys. Best of all, were two badger setts in the bank above the lake.

Nobody was ever allowed to disturb them and the occupants grew used to the presence of Man, because the path, which passed between them, wandered through the shade of lovely beech and oak woods, and returned by the river, which played a different tune for every passing storm. So many visitors loved this walk that, instead of cowering in terror below ground, the badgers grew blasé and took no notice.

We used to go down to the sett after tea, light a scrap of paper with a match, and watch the smoke eddy and swirl as it smouldered.

Badgers are incredibly clever – or lucky? – in the way they site their setts. They are often on the side of a hill or bank, or in a clearing in woodland, where they can tunnel straight in.

Wherever they are the currents of air seem to eddy around, instead of drifting across in a single direction, no matter which way the wind is blowing.

We repeatedly found that the most obvious place to choose for an observation post was in the very spot where our scent would have drifted directly towards the sett and given the badgers the exact warning they wanted.

So we watched the smoke trail and picked a place to sit where our taint would drift away and not betray us.

If there were tunnels, connecting the two setts, they would have passed directly beneath the path, but the badgers had grown so used to almost continuous human footfalls that they took no notice. In summer time, when we were there, they were usually out well before dusk, and often before I would have expected them, even in remote and undisturbed country.

The bank fell so steeply away down to the lake that we got an uninterrupted view as they went down to dig their latrines and to drink. Then the dry undergrowth would crackle like a bonfire as the cubs fluffed out their fur and blundered round in tomboy games of tag.

Their fur stuck out so far that their undulating gambols gave a strange illusion of weightlessness, and they appeared to float around as easily as tight blown, gassy balloons.

One of the greatest of the old school Nature photographers lived just outside Builth Wells, a few miles away, and he had pioneered the art of flash photography, when illumination was achieved by igniting a magnesium flare, and he regarded modern electronic flash equipment

as an invention of the Devil. He said that it had taken
the art out of wildlife photography and that any fool
could do as well with electronic flash as an expert could.

Much of his early work had been done with badgers
and he pointed to a telltale dark patch in front of most
of the models in his early pictures.

This was a patch of treacle, poured on the ground
to persuade his subjects to take up their pose on the
precise spot where he had pre-focused his camera.

I might say that treacle is an invaluable aid to badger
watching too. Sweet things are as irresistible to them as
they are to bears. A patch of treacle, renewed daily, will
often persuade a whole colony to move their playground
from thick cover to the best adjacent spot for a watcher
to see them.

The first glimpse of the evening is often a striped
snout delicately testing the breeze for the taint of
intruders. Within seconds, the patriarch of the colony
will be sitting on the bank, enjoying the luxury of a
meditative scratch.

Although there is much to be learned from watching
them, such badger watching does have its limitations.

It is impossible to see what they are doing when once
the light has faded, when they have wandered into cover
or over the brow of the nearest bank. The next time
there will be anything of interest to see, will be when
they return to the sett at first light.

The other snag to consistent badger watching is that
the very people who would most like to take their
pleasure this uncomfortable way, are often those who
live furthest from a sett.

I know farmers, with several setts on their land, who
see badgers less often than townsfolk who have to motor
miles. When they do arrive, the wind may be wrong,

the weather miserable, or their quarry may have been previously disturbed.

The only alternative I could see was to keep a badger for myself.

There are major pitfalls in trying to deduce facts about animals from the way tame or captive specimens behave.

The wits of hand-reared animals may never have been sharpened by hunger or danger and the fact that they have no fear of Man obviously colours their reactions to human strangers.

I have first-hand experience of how necessary it is to treat such discoveries with reserve, because I have spent twenty-five years with semi-captive creatures, since the only contact I could get with our native animals, in their wild state, was at week-ends and on holiday.

I have tamed various birds, a stoat, weasels and even a common brown rat. But the one which gave me most pleasure, mixed with remorse, was the badger I had for ten years.

I wanted one for a long time and at last I went to see Bert Gripton, who made his living, directly and indirectly, from working terriers. I asked him to keep me the next badger cub he got.

At that time, Bert acknowledged no man as master, living an almost gipsy life breeding and training and selling terriers.

His shop window was the arena provided when the local hunt got into difficulties. When their fox escaped hounds and went to ground, Bert would be on hand with spade and terrier, to make him show his mask again. For this he got a small retainer and a few shillings for each fox he bolted.

Interested – and critical – spectators were always at

hand to express opinions on the working qualities of his dogs, and, since he didn't tolerate second raters out in public, attempts were often made to persuade him to part with a successful dog.

'I'm sorry,' he'd say, 'but that's the best dog in England. I make my living from him, but I'll sell you a pup by him.'

If his potential customer let his enthusiasm run away with him, and pushed the price too far above market value, Bert was persuaded, very much against his will of course, to make a 'sacrifice' and part with the dog!

The one he brought out next week, to replace it, automatically succeeded to the title 'Best in England'.

The fact is that Bert, himself, was certainly the best man in England that I ever saw at producing good working terriers. He often had thirty or forty in his kennels and not only knew every fox earth and badger sett for miles around, he even claimed to be able to identify individual foxes by sight.

He was supposed to do a job of earth stopping the night before the meet – as part of the work for his retainer – but he was never very keen. It was better for his trade if the fox did get to ground so that potential customers could assess the skill of his dogs when he was told to bolt it.

It therefore followed that he wasn't very fond of badgers. The best dog in the world won't bolt a badger, so it always meant a tedious dig to retrieve his dog and account for the badger. This often meant the disappearance of a bored customer before he'd done a deal.

So Bert accounted for what brocks he could so that he could leave maximum accommodation for foxes. He didn't waste his efforts because there was a ready market for badger cubs, and, on 22 February 1951, he rang me up to ask me to fetch the cub I'd ordered.

I understood his hurry, when I saw him. He was small enough to lie on the palm of my hand and just tipped our kitchen scale at a pound and a quarter. His little piggy eyes were barely open and, though his back was grey with young hair, his belly was still naked and smooth. His face was already white, with two black stripes running down to his white tipped ears, and his leathery feet were armed with needle-sharp claws.

The most disturbing thing about him was a shallow gash along his shoulder and back. It hadn't quite penetrated the tough hide, but I wondered if the terrier which inflicted it had done any internal damage as well.

I suffered a fleeting twinge of conscience when it occurred to me that this young brock might still be suckling its dam, in the depths of a sett, if I hadn't offered to buy him. Perhaps the death of the sow and the rest of the litter was chalked up to my account?

Then I supposed that they would have been dug out anyway and that the cub would have been unlikely to have had such a good home anywhere else. Nothing is more easily deceived than the human conscience! I almost got round to believing I was doing a worthwhile job in saving him. Always provided, of course, that I managed to rear him.

The first thing he needed was not food but warmth. I stuffed him into my shirt, next to my skin, to keep him comfortable till I got him home. After the first few instinctive, painful efforts to dig himself deeper in, he settled down and snuggled quiet and still.

By the time we got back he seemed to have accepted me as Mum, albeit a dry one, and resented being hauled out into the light again.

I fitted him up with an extremely simple but effective

nursery. It was a wooden box, just large enough to take two large, flat cigarette tins, side by side on the floor.

I stretched a sock over each tin and put a 15-watt pigmy electric bulb in one of them. This kept it at about blood temperature and, when the cub was cold, he lay on this heated bed, which was as soft and warm as his mother's belly.

When he got too warm, all he had to do was to crawl to the other end of the wooden box and lie on the sock which covered the empty tin.

Two simple tins in a wooden box, with soft wool or flannel covers to lie on, make a most effective incubator, never too cold and never too hot, and I have reared all sorts of young creatures with it.

Nothing is normally easier than a badger, because he starts off with the advantage of enormous toughness. But this cub really was too young to have been parted from his mother, and I had a job to feed him.

His mouth was too small for a normal baby's teat, so that I had to fall back on the rubber teat from a doll's bottle. It was flimsy rubber, unperforated, and had obviously been designed more for ornament than use.

I don't usually worry if young things refuse to feed the first few hours because I know from experience that their growing hunger will soon persuade them to be sensible.

This cub was really too young to leave for long, so my wife tried frequently to get him to feed while I was out, but the best luck she had was to persuade him to take a little baby food from an eye dropper.

It was just enough to maintain the spark of life, and within twenty-four hours his hunger had conquered his resistance to change of diet. Next time I went, he chattered with anticipation at the first whiff of food and took it freely from his doll's teat.

Perhaps 'freely' is an overstatement. He was always a very slow feeder and would often take up to forty-five minutes to finish a meal.

This had important side effects. Between us, my wife and I were spending up to three hours a day feeding our badger cub, and it gave us time to get to know each other pretty well. Plenty of time!

We were delighted to see his first eye open and amused when the other took a couple of days longer, imparting a most sinister leer. His warm belly, which always felt wet, when it was naked, furred up and he suddenly became a perfect miniature badger.

By this time he had grown enough for us to discard the doll's teats and replace them with standard teats from baby's bottles, which are already perforated.

The size of perforation proved very important. If the holes were too small, he found the milk difficult to suck and flew into a furious temper, chattering with rage and frustration, until he was physically exhausted.

If the liquid flowed too freely, he spluttered and choked and refused to feed at all. Trial, error, perseverance and luck triumphed, in the end, and Bloody Bill Brock grew almost visibly.

In the sett, the sow keeps the cubs groomed and it is obviously easy and natural to lick their hind parts while their other ends are firmly attached to the teats. This anal stimulation produces a reflex evacuation of the cubs' bowels and very young cubs often seem incapable of emptying themselves at all without such stimulation.

The droppings are charged with a substance in which the dam is deficient, so the natural reaction is to eat them. This is Nature's way of keeping the nest clean until the young are old enough to leave the sett when they want to relieve themselves.

We soon found, however, that keeping our cub's bowels in order wasn't simply a matter of physical stimulus, applied to produce a reflex response.

The baby-food mixture had to have the precise amounts of sugar or limewater needed to produce the result. Additional sugar cured constipation and, if we overdid it and got him too loose, limewater added to subsequent feeds would soon put matters right.

Always provided, of course, that we added the right amount. I know of no text books written to give detailed instructions in these matters and, as the effect of either treatment often took several hours to work, it was rather a matter of hit or miss.

Our young brock was a very tough chap and seemed to thrive on our early mistakes. As he grew stronger he fed more quickly and then wanted to play as soon as he had blunted the edge of his hunger.

He associated us with food and warmth and had already developed a powerful fixation for human beings, showing his delight the moment either of us appeared.

His play was very rough. The same sort of mock fighting puppies enjoy, partly to test and develop his teeth and partly so that attack and defence, practised often enough, would be automatic when the time of real need arrived.

Even at that tender age, he loved to dig. His blunt snout would explore the palm of my hand or fold in my clothing and, with no warning whatever, two powerful paws would try to dig a passage through whatever obstruction was baulking him.

At this stage, he never bit hard enough to break the skin, but his needle-sharp teeth and claws could be very painful indeed.

Although badgers are naturally such companionable creatures, there was no difficulty about returning him to his box in the early stages. He was always so pleasantly replete that he was ready to fall asleep after half an hour's rough and tumble.

When he grew too large for his original box, I transferred him to a loosebox in the stable, where he could still have his electrically warmed bed, but where there was room for him to get exercise when he was rested and ready for play.

As he grew up, which he did with miraculous speed, he needed less sleep and more and more exercise. However hungry he was when I went to feed him, it was always fuss that he craved more than food, and he would not eat until we had demonstrated our mutual affection.

By the time he was as big as a cat, he would follow anywhere I went and developed a disconcerting habit of getting between my feet, rearing up against my legs, in the hope that I would pick him up and make much of him. When I put him down, he would attack my ankles, in mock fury, and I had to goose step to safety.

His habit of following at heel was not training but a natural precaution against getting lost. He was so short-sighted that I do not believe he could distinguish a stationary object at more than a few feet range. His hearing and nose were superb, but he was so unsure of himself on strange territory that he tried to keep so close to me that our contact was almost physical.

He loved the dogs, though they soon found him rather rough, and he would chase them across the field, keeping up with an undulating gait, like a little rocking-horse.

During such periods of excitement, his fur would stand out stiff as a chimney sweep's brush, and he pretended to bite the dogs' feet, shooting his snout out from beneath his front leg, with the speed of a viper's strike.

This stretched the pad of powerful muscle over his neck and shoulders, so that he seemed impervious to the dogs' retribution.

Their feet were very sensitive to such boisterous play, and they were always the first to break off the engagement and retreat far faster than he could follow.

If you like laughing *at* misfortune, his consternation at being left was very funny. His back arched, like a frightened cat, and he stood on tiptoe, to make himself more formidable and to widen his horizon, his coat standing out to twice its size.

But there was nothing funny in his plight. He really was afraid and he froze motionless, so that he could hear the faintest sound of movement, either by the dogs or me. Meanwhile, his delicate nose tested every eddy for the slightest clue.

My guilty conscience plagued me for teasing him and I called to him because I loved to watch the sinuous grace as he rocketed towards me, and the warmth of his greeting gave us equal delight.

Occasionally I kept silent and motionless, to see what he would do. When he had waited as long as he dared for some sound or smell that he recognized, he worked round in a circle, exactly as a pointer would do.

Sooner or later, he was bound to finish directly downwind of me or the dogs and then, quite overjoyed, he thundered towards us.

It was a good example of the reserve necessary in evaluating reactions of creatures which are not truly wild.

A wild badger would not normally get himself so easily lost and nor would mine if he had not been so obsessed with the idea that lay in keeping near to me.

Every badger has a musk gland near his anus (as do

all other members of the Mustilidae), and badgers never wander far on strange land without squatting, as if in deep meditation. This is really to 'spot' a minute drop of musk every few yards to mark the territory they cover.

When they want to return, all that is necessary is to 'hunt' their own line of spots back to the point of departure.

It would be very difficult to observe, in the wild, just how a badger did navigate back to base in the unlikely event of getting lost in strange territory, with no musk trail to guide him. My tame one, when left to forage naturally, as opposed to playing with the dogs till he forgot his natural caution, would always give a wonderful demonstration of navigation by musk spots.

By September, he was more than half-grown and as rough in his play as the most badly trained boisterous bull terrier.

For many people, his enchantment would have evaporated entirely. This becomes obvious every autumn from the number of people who have reared cubs and want to be rid of them. They bombard me with every excuse from theirs being the exceptional 'rogue badger', to the unforeseen high cost of keeping him or the sensitivity of their kids to a little rough play. A few even tell the truth and say that the novelty has worn off, but I am impartially unsympathetic with all.

Badgers which have been kindly treated, regularly handled and given proper companionship, do not grow suddenly savage, though ignorant people may confuse roughness with viciousness.

Bill's play grew so rough that he drew blood on my hands and wrists most evenings, not because he was nasty tempered but because I was more tender and effete than most badgers would have been, and they should have been his natural playmates.

Living in a stable loosebox and just coming out with the dogs and me at evening time, simply did not give him enough exercise to work off his surplus energy. The rough housing he gave us was a simple yardstick on my deficiency in keeping him too closely confined.

To some small degree, I alleviated this by hanging an old motor-cycle tyre from a strong tension spring, hung from the room of his loosebox. The tyre hung down so that its lowest edge was about six inches above the stable floor and, when Bill bumbled into it, it swung away and returned to nudge him.

When he gripped it with his teeth, the spring imparted a sense of liveliness. The more he tugged it, the more it tugged back, and he amused himself for hours wrestling with it and rolling through it as if it had been another cub.

It was a trick I had seen in the days when they used to get bull terriers fit for fighting, and a keen dog would worry and shake a hunk of leather or tyre, hung from a spring, till they were ready to drop.

Bill did not take his pleasures as hard as that, but he did amuse himself a great deal and I suppose it supplied a little of the exercise he so badly needed. But he never deluded himself that it was another badger or really alive at all. The instant he heard me, he would always leave it and come sniffing under the door, whinnying his affectionate welcome.

Badgers are such companionable creatures that it was wicked to sentence him to this solitary confinement, without giving him enough exercise to send him to sleep with exhaustion when he got home.

This became more and more obvious from the very

difficulty of confining him at all. The stable was brick built, with stone sett floor. The door was split in halves, the top always being open for light and air, because he was quite unable to leap up even the twelve inches necessary to reach the top of the lower half.

Although his back legs were comparatively weak (his action always reminded me of a hedgehog, when he was walking directly away), his shoulders and forelegs had prodigious power.

When I shut him in the stable, he would lie on his side and scratch for hours on end at the crack where the door closed. It was sound, solid Victorian woodwork and his claws were as blunt as a dog's, though far stronger.

The door was no match for him and soon began to splinter so that I had to line it with steel sheet, which was too smooth to give any purchase, before I could contain him. Even this didn't deter him and he thumped that old door hour after hour, night after night, partly as an exercise routine and partly because he never gave up trying to get to us.

It wasn't the captivity which worried him. If the bolt on his door worked loose with the vibration, and let him out, as it often did, he was not in the least interested in the freedom of the outside world. He simply came to join us in the house.

This was a mixed blessing. We would have given him the freedom of the house with the greatest of pleasure, but he simply was not fitted for domesticity.

His instinct of cleanliness was almost clinical and he needed none of the conventional house training a puppy does. It simply never crossed his mind to make a mess in the house and he never emptied himself except in a latrine pit he had dug.

The snag was his inexhaustible energy. He was never still for a minute, except to lie on our laps to have his tummy scratched. Otherwise his restlessness was always dominant, and he treated any obstacles to his progress, such as closed doors, with the vigorous intolerance that he treated the door of his stable. But the doors in the house did not have the advantage of steel sheeting.

If a spring in an arm-chair creaked, he ripped the cover in case it was a mouse, and he gave the dogs no peace, although, having more exercise than he did, they wanted to relax by the fire when they came indoors, and were bored with his continuous invitations to play.

He turned the place into such Bedlam that we could only have him in when we were completely free to give him our undivided attention. We enjoyed this as much as he did but it did have its limitations and it was never enough for him although we gave him much more time than we could spare.

However inconvenient it might be, we never missed a day having him in the house or taking him out for exercise during his whole life, except when we were on holiday. And that was never for more than a week in the whole year.

Expeditions which would correspond to walks for the dogs were very rewarding. It wasn't such fun on strange ground because of his phobia about being lost, which concentrated his whole attention on keeping near the dogs or us, to bolster his sense of security.

If he did lose contact, it was pathetic, because he was as distraught as a stray dog which has been cast out in a callous world. No loneliness could be more poignant nor terror more rigid, yet he never lost his sense of dignity. He didn't lose control of his feelings till the moment of ecstasy when he found us again.

We spent a great deal of time in the fields and allotments opposite the house so that he could become intimate enough with their geography to head unhesitatingly for home whenever he wanted.

He spotted so many of his musk trails over the whole area that, though it must all have smelt familiar, it was difficult to see how he unravelled the line through such a maze of plenty. Yet he was too shortsighted to see the landmarks, sound didn't help, but he had an unerring instinct for direction, when once he had marked it out with his spots.

His worst period was that first September, when he was about seven months old. He didn't know his own strength and his boisterous buffoonery was rather a bore, and strangers could be excused from believing he was reverting to the savage wild.

He gradually grew out of it and became gentler so all that was subsequently necessary was the ability to decide who he disliked – and respect him for it.

Most strangers did not interest him one way or another. He would go up to them, sniff at them as a dog would, and frequently turn his back and squat on the nearest foot. This was simply marking them, by tainting them with his musk, so that other badgers would know that they were henceforth part of his territory.

Occasionally, he disliked someone on sight (or more probably at scent), and the most common category to incur such displeasure were press photographers.

I never discovered if this was because he knew, instinctively, that they were about to produce an electronic flash gun or whether they emanate some brash odour of intrusion.

If I disturbed his daytime slumbers and lifted him out of his straw-filled box, his nature was so sweet that he positively crooned with delight.

When I carried him for an introduction to most visitors, he was impersonally polite and displayed neither pleasure nor antipathy.

Yet, if it was a press photographer, I would feel his muscles go tense and rigid with anxiety and, if I put him down, he would hurry rudely home.

Once or twice, I was persuaded to fetch him out again, but he would not even let me lift him from his box. His back would arch and he would put his head between his forelegs. If I was stupid enough to persist in putting my hands around his belly then, he would bite them.

Not viciously, at first, but far too hard for comfort. He would sometimes hold them in this iron grip for two or three minutes, pinning me, doubled-up, as surely as if I had sprung a rabbit gin set in the bottom of his box.

If I had persisted then, I do not doubt that he would have mauled me seriously.

I never blamed him in the least. Experience with handling wild animals indicates the safety margin, which is only exceeded at peril. Only fools would have incited him to the point where he would have had to sacrifice his dignity to submit, and we knew each other well enough to develop a deep mutual respect.

Failure to recognize such danger signals is all that has earned badgers a false reputation for uncertain tempers.

I have found that very few animals *suddenly* turn savage. There is normally fair warning for all who have eyes to read the signs. Those who push their luck, whether in ignorance or bravado, ask for all they get.

So many factors combined to indicate how irksome confinement must be, that we seriously thought of setting our captive free.

We were put off, not so much by his dependence on

us for food as by the almost psychopathic fixation he had developed for humanity in general, and me in particular. He was genuinely miserable when set down in strange surroundings, with only himself for company.

We decided that the least we could do was to shoulder the responsibility we had assumed and, for the next nine and a half years, we did our best to make his life as pleasant as we could.

I fed him every night and amused myself testing his preferences by offering a wide variety of food and observing what he selected first.

I tried eggs, whole and broken, bread and milk, bread and treacle, poultry, rabbits, rats, fruit cake, potatoes and cooked and raw meat.

There was never any hesitation about taking sweet things first. He always chose bread-and-treacle, cake or anything with honey.

Then he took the eggs, though partly, I think, because he loved to hear the shells crunch. Meat and poultry were at the bottom of the list and I even tried putting in a hen the moment after I had dislocated its neck.

It flopped about with the reflex convulsions which follow sudden, violent death, and Bill was very interested. He followed it round, by sound, nuzzling it when he got up to it. If it had been alive, it would have had time to escape ten times over. As it was he nudged it repeatedly until he eventually decided that it was edible and finally bit it.

When I took him in the field, he ate any earthworms stupid enough to go out courting in the evening dew, and any beetles or larvae he came across.

He regarded the great, bumbling black dor beetles, which fly on summer nights, and often dig under dry cowpats, as an especial delicacy.

I had to be careful to keep him out of the garden because he found bulbs irresistible and was too keen to dig up plants or to make holes in the lawn – just in case there was something tasty hidden at the roots.

As one would expect with a young creature growing so fast, his appetite, that first autumn, was prodigious. But, late in December, we had a nasty shock. Without any warning at all, he suddenly ceased to feed. Not entirely, but he only ate at intervals of several days.

Each night, I offered something more tempting than the night before, and next morning, when it had not been touched, I gave it to the dogs or poultry or ferrets, depending on what it was.

At about the same time, he developed a nasty, dry cough, and the local vet, who preferred to prescribe from a safe distance, was not unduly helpful.

There was no question of hibernation, because, each night, when I went to see him, he came to greet me with his usual whinny of affection but, though his delight in our meeting was undiminished, his appetite for food was negligible.

This condition persisted for about five weeks, after which his normal appetite gradually returned, and it was repeated at the same time of year for the rest of his life. His cough, which soon cleared up, did not seem to have any connection with the loss of appetite, and never recurred.

At about this time, I had the first of two wonderfully tame weasels. This one lived in the house and used to lie up in an old sock, which he greatly preferred to any type of material we tried in his nest box.

When I wanted him, I used to poke a finger into this sock and he replied by greeting me with a high-pitched crooning purr of delight. I was particularly interested by this because I had come across no reference to any sound made by weasels except their normal chatter of alarm, pain or rage.

I recorded the sound on a tape-recorder and inadvertently played it back at half speed.

This halved the frequency and lowered the pitch and the resulting sound was almost indistinguishable from the whinny of affection that badgers make.

It has, of course, long been known that both badgers and weasels belong to the family Mustilidae, and that both have musk glands near their anus. But it was interesting to discover, by the fluke of replaying a recording at half speed, that they almost speak the same language too.

Although he lived with us for almost ten years, Bloody Bill Brock showed no sign of developing ill temper or becoming savage with increasing age.

He was often very rough to handle, simply because his inadequate exercise made him abnormally lively, and, as he got older, he grew less reticent about expressing dislike of some strangers. But he always made this perfectly plain so that I had fair warning that he would not tolerate being picked up, once he had met someone he didn't approve of.

I thought none the worse of him for it. It simply meant that our mutual respect grew as strong as our mutual affection.

In the winter, when he was ten, he went off his food as usual. I wasn't worried because it had happened, with no ill effects, nine times before.

This time he lost more weight than usual, and nothing I offered him tempted him for many days on end. His coat grew harsh and I fancied his eyes were not so bright.

An unmistakable symptom of old age, in most carnivorae, is deterioration of the teeth, but his were sound and white, with no visible signs of decay.

Nevertheless, the loss of appetite really was abnormal – even for the time of year – and his coat was normally so much brighter and his eyes more brilliant that I began to assume he had reached his natural span.

He was still as pleased to see me when I called, but no longer boisterous or rough.

Then, as I was fondling him, one night, I noticed a swelling under his jaw, no bigger than a garden pea. I examined it more closely and found that it exuded a sticky fluid and, when I smelt my finger, I recognized the familiar pong which ferrets give off a few days after they have been mauled by a rat.

Suspecting that the swelling was a small abscess, which might account for the abnormal loss of appetite, I contacted the vet.

He was not the man who had funked prescribing for Bill's cough, and he gave me some antibiotic ointment and asked me to try it before we got down to anything more drastic.

It did the trick, for a bit, and Bill came back on to his food for a week or so, before the symptoms recurred.

Then the abscess burst and the pain seemed to subside, because he began to feed normally again. The relief proved to be only temporary and it became clear that the trouble must be deep seated, and I could see that the old fellow was suffering considerably.

I asked the vet to operate and establish the real cause of the trouble, but it was the first badger that he had been asked to treat and he was loth to take the risk as he frankly admitted that he was not certain what strength of anaesthetic to use.

I thought that, if he could not be cured, it was kinder to kill him, and so I had my way.

The amount of anaesthetic needed to make that tough old brock relinquish consciousness was incredible. Far more than would have been lethal to larger animals. The results of the examination were extremely depressing. The trouble arose from a deep-seated condition of the jaw bone and had spread to the whole of the base of the tongue.

The verdict was that the operation would entail major surgery, with a painful convalescence. Even then, the cure was likely to be no more than temporary.

So we did the only merciful thing and did not allow him to recover from the anaesthetic.

I went home heavy at heart, not because I had lost my badger, which had been almost a member of the family for ten years all but a month. I was sad because I was conscious that he had never led a really full life and that he must often have been lonely and bored.

I had learned the lesson the hard way for both of us. Badgers should never be kept alone or in captivity.

I made a firm resolve never to keep another.

CHAPTER THREE

The Vacant Setts

Within a few years of Bloody Bill's death, my whole circumstances had altered and it became possible to work at home, earning my living with my pen. Until then, I had wasted my life, doing long and regular hours all week in a factory to earn enough money to do the things I wanted to do, in what spare time was left.

We were able to move to deep country and bought ninety acres of derelict woodland in the middle of an estate which had been broken up by death duties.

The prospect was entrancing because the wood already had a small heronry, wild fallow deer, all sorts of exciting woodland birds, foxes – and badgers!

Our first summer was one long safari – on our own place. We compiled a list of the creatures which shared it with us and soon found that, although badgers enjoyed our hospitality at night, they went elsewhere to spend their days.

As soon as we got to know our neighbours, we begged leave to explore their land for setts. It was apparent that there were a good number of wild badgers in the district and we found four setts within a mile radius and the Forestry Commission Game Warden said that there were several more in the thousand-odd acres of wood which joined up to us.

But none were on our land. Our soil is heavy, cold clay, and, over the brow of the hill, where the land drops away to a brook, there is an outcrop of warm, well-drained sandy gravel.

One neighbour had a very itchy trigger finger and made no bones about the fact that he shot any badger he saw, and I suspected that shooting was not the only means he used.

He has since gone and his successor simply asks that I keep the badgers from one sett on his farm, where they undermine an arable field and are a danger to farm implements. This is the sett I stink out regularly with Reynardine.

The fact that badgers were unwelcome, locally, where they had chosen to settle but would have been honoured guests on our land, put obvious ideas in my head. I decided, since they didn't like digging in our cold clay, that I would dig an artificial earth myself in the hopes that they would accept my invitation and settle here.

A pool of an acre and a half comes to within eighty yards of the house and the far side melts into the wood.

This far bank slopes up very steeply about ten feet up from the water's edge so I chose what I hoped would be the ideal spot for a sett, close to an open ride we can see from the house. Success would mean that every badger using the sett would have to cross the ride in full view of the house, but far enough away not to be worried by us.

Long before I had finished digging, my sympathies were all with the badgers. There was about six inches of soft leafmould, built up over the generations from the oak leaves which fell every autumn. Below that was two foot six of brown, cloying clay on top of a foot of pebbles, twice as big as tennis balls.

It was glutinous enough to suck tight wellington boots off, after a spell of wet weather, and I convinced myself that there was no tougher digging, however far I searched.

Below the cobble-stones was a band of green marl, in comparison with which the brown stuff nearer the surface, was soft and sweet as face cream. I dug two hours a day for over a week, but when I was done I was pleased with my handiwork.

I made an oak plank kennel, two feet by three feet by eighteen inches deep, with the top six inches below ground level.

Leading from it, for entrance or exit, were two tunnels dropping sharp away to surface above the pool.

A conventional artificial fox earth has a tunnel leading in one side of the chamber and out the other, with the entrances as far away from each other as possible. The idea is that a terrier can enter by one pipe, rattle the fox around his sleeping quarters and bolt him through the other.

I feared that, if I was successful with my sett, the Hunt or other terrier owners might come when I was out and undo all the good work I had done, so I modified the traditional design.

I piped two deep trenches, in the shape of a letter Y, connecting only the single pipe to the chamber. My idea was that there would be two entrances, at ground level, but that they would converge so that only one would enter the chamber.

It would then be impossible for more than one dog at a time to approach the badgers, which would be safe from behind and have only one pipe to defend. They would thus be quite impregnable from the best terrier and it would be impossible to get at them without actually removing the top of the sett.

My theory was never put to the test because no badgers ever took up residence in what I regarded as an eminently desirable dwelling. I put straws and twigs across the entrance to the pipes, to give me the clue when anything was interested, but, though they were often moved, there were no local latrines and the 'padding' indicated that visits were only casual and that no badger took up permanent residence.

It is easy to be wise after the event, but it took me a very long time to discover what a stupid thing I'd done.

Artificial fox earths do not have the pipe entering one side and leaving the other only for the convenience of the terriers. The other vital purpose is to direct a flow of fresh air through to ensure adequate ventilation.

The single entrance from my Y pipe encouraged no decent airflow and, when I opened the chamber up, to have a look what had happened, I found the whole bedding soggy and mouldy. So I remedied the defect by putting in a vertical 'chimney' from the chamber, and waited patiently to see what happened.

About a mile away, a major agricultural operation was in progress to reclaim a thousand acres of derelict parkland for agriculture. It was necessary to put in drains, four feet deep and a chain apart, over the whole area, and to plough and lime it to get a seedbed good enough to grow anything but the indigenous feg or reed or bracken.

Before this could be done, it was necessary to winch out many hundreds of venerable old trees and blow up the roots or burn them.

One of the most famous of these trees was the Squitch Oak, which was reputed to have lived through more than a thousand summers.

The top had long since been blown out, or struck by lightning and, even in those days, the old tree had been regarded so highly that the jagged branches had been neatly sawn off and plated with lead sheet, to keep out the wet and rot.

The man who looked after ley cattle, in the park, told me that a litter of fox cubs had been reared under this tree as long as he could remember and that he had an idea that there were badgers there too.

The time came to grub it up, in the name of agricultural progress, but it was too stocky and thick and strong to pull out with a wire hawser and mechanical winch. Nothing short of dynamite would shift it.

By this time it was widely known, in the district, that I was prepared to go to unusual lengths to save any badger I could, so the farm manager called to say they were going to blow up the Squitch Oak, so what could be done about the badgers underneath?

The obvious thing was to stink them out with Reynardine so that they had left before the tree was sent sky high. There were only two or three open holes to the sett, so I reckoned nothing could put up with the stink I left for more than a few hours.

I hadn't reckoned on the devotion of a nursing sow. The cubs must have been about three weeks old and the parents opened up the holes almost as soon as I'd blocked them and were obviously bravely determined to stick it out till the cubs were large enough to move.

It would be unreasonable to expect commercially minded farmers to hold up the whole of a major operation for the sake of a family of badgers who are obstinately determined not to take the hint that they have outstayed their welcome.

This lot were lucky. My neighbour is exceptionally tolerant and simply asked me to think again.

So I ask my friend the terrier man, who had dug out Bloody Bill Brock, if he would come over and have a day's badger digging. I told him it looked a simple sett to work and that we could bag the whole family and transfer them to the sett I'd dug in my wood.

I made square wooden bungs to fit the end of the pipes so that there would be plenty of air but no room to escape. Then I prepared a huge bowl of bread-and-treacle so that I could fasten the whole lot in my sett, and keep them fastened in for forty-eight hours.

By that time, I hoped, they could have settled down and the Squitch Oak would have been blown harmlessly out of the ground so that they would find their old home gone, if they did try to return. And, since it was less than a mile away, it would be 'home' territory to them and they should have a better chance of accepting it.

Never count your badgers before you catch them. We started to dig about half past nine on Sunday morning. Or, to be more precise, we put the first terrier in. Within two minutes we heard her 'speaking' below ground and saw a badger pass across the mouth of the main entrance. So there is no doubt whatever that there were badgers there.

As soon as the terrier had settled to one spot, we started to dig and, considering how small the sett seemed, the little dog's song of hate sounded a mighty long way off.

It turned out to be an exceptionally large sett and I imagine the explanation for its deceptive size was that it had been gassed in the past, and that subsequent badgers had not bothered to open up all the holes when they returned.

I can think of no other explanation for such a labyrinth of underground passages, served by so few holes. There were not only a lot of passages, but they went exceptionally deep into the sandy bank as well.

About ten of us took it in turns to dig, and the trenches we dug were five or six feet deep and tortuous enough to have provided cover for an army. The one bright spot was that there was a press photographer and television cameraman there and it was so cold that, since there were no pictures to take, they mucked in with the spades to prevent the marrow freezing in their bones. I've never seen press men work so hard.

It was a friendly party and nobody minded – at first. It aroused latent hunting instincts that had been quite unsuspected and, for those who were reluctant to harass badgers by digging them out with dogs, at least there was a sense of purpose. If we didn't dig them out, they would certainly be blown up.

By dinner time, we were getting tired and caked with an emulsion of sweat and sand, which penetrated hair and eyes and clothes, but the voice of the terrier was only another six feet in, so triumph was at hand.

Just as the terrier's tail came into view, the badger charged and the dog popped out, like a cork from a bottle and wisely decided to call it a day.

By the time another terrier had been fetched from the van, the badger had moved and we were back where we started.

Some of the diggers sloped off towards the local, before closing time, and the hard core started again, laboriously digging towards the faint yapping, which was elusive as a will-o'-the-wisp.

I would never have credited that muscles could have tolerated such misuse, or that the human frame was proof against such agony. We dug interminably, always approaching our goal but never arriving. By the time the second dog copied his mate and packed it in, our network of trenches had escalated from platoon to brigade proportions.

We lost the battle in the end, and I do not believe that we were as near 'our' badgers when darkness fell as we had been ten minutes after we started. That one, fleeting glimpse of our quarry was all we got all day.

So we followed the terriers' example and gave them best, returning home dead beat, hungry, aching and with empty bags.

Our abortive dig had one good effect. The poor creatures, which had put up with the powerful, synthetic stink of Reynardine, could not tolerate such close proximity to us.

They, too, called it a day and had left the sett the next time I went round. So I filled in the holes and, when they were not disturbed for two more days, I knew that they must have taken their cubs too, so it was safe for the tree removers to come and demolish the old Squitch Oak.

I shall never know if the badgers would ever have used my artificial sett because I wanted a larger fox-proof area for my wild ducks and roe deer. I included the sett in the area surrounded by six-foot netting, so that it was no longer accessible to creatures outside the perimeter fence.

That didn't mean that I gave up the struggle to persuade badgers to reside in our wood.

There were two ancient, stag-headed oaks between the house and the pool, and every interesting wild fowl, which joined our resident flock, inevitably landed out of sight behind them.

We hate chopping trees down and much prefer to leave them and plant young ones to replace them when they die. But these two oaks had only been spared in a major felling, thirty years before, because they were too decrepit to be of any commercial value, even then. So, with some misgiving, we felled them to open up the view of the pool from the house. We persuaded one of the bulldozer drivers, who was tree clearing in the park, to come and move the roots when we had cut off the trunks for firewood.

He bulldozed them into a pile, at the edge of the wood, and covered them with a blanket of soil, which I sowed with grass seed.

By spring, all that was to be seen, from the house, was a pleasant green mound at the edge of the wood, which I was convinced would be irresistible to badgers.

There must be a multitude of dry caverns among the huge pile of roots, and once the grass roots matted, the whole would be dry as tinder. Any creature wanting to use it, could approach from the cover of the wood behind and there was water, within a few yards, in the ditch which feeds the pool.

Muzzling my curiosity, I took care not to approach more than about once a fortnight, and was soon delighted to find that a number of creatures were investigating.

The vegetation around was padded by both badgers and foxes but neither made any regular tracks underneath.

The fallow deer loved it, too. They have an entrancing habit of playing 'king-of-the-castle' as lambs do, and we sat for hours in the evening watching them rushing up and down the steep sides.

They were timid and elusive, when we came, because any deer which showed its nose was asking for a charge of shot, in those days. But, since we have been here, they have changed entirely.

We leave a stand of timber, about seventeen acres next

to the house, entirely undisturbed. I go in at the end of winter, to shoot any grey squirrels before the nesting season, and again, in May, to count the herons' nests. I try to avoid going in for any other reason, so that it has come to be regarded, by our local wildlife community, as an inviolable sanctuary.

I walk along the rides, which form its boundary, several times a day, with the dogs, but, because none of us enter that part of the wood, the herons and deer, especially, have acquired an unusual sense of security.

It is possible to walk within fifteen or twenty yards of the wild deer without disturbing them in the least, and I throw a little maize in the ride behind me as I go.

Within minutes of my passing, the deer come out in the open, in front of the windows, to feed on the corn or to lick the lumps of rock salt I have placed at strategic positions. These deer found the badger sett we'd constructed from tree roots more of an attraction than the badgers did.

Whenever we went out at dusk or dawn, we usually saw badgers feeding in the wood, but, as they were not 'our' badgers, it was not what I wanted.

I felt that, living in the heart of what was obviously such suitable country for them, it ought to be possible to persuade them to take up residence where we could watch from the house whenever they were out and about.

Most people, who have done work with wild badgers, have had to go some distance to where the badgers lived and were limited to observations made within the times they could arrange.

I was determined to create conditions attractive enough to persuade Mahomet to come to the mountain. I was convinced that the only thing preventing badgers living – as opposed to feeding – in our wood was the fact that the soil was unsuitable for them to dig a sett.

This might be to my eventual advantage. If ours had been hospitable, well-drained soil, the odds were that the badgers would have established setts in the most inaccessible places to observe them.

My object was to create ideal conditions in the precise spots where I could see exactly what happened, and I was convinced that, once they had accepted one of my sites, the seclusion from disturbance and ideal feeding would ensure that it would be continuously occupied. The problem was making the initial breakthrough.

A chance eventually came. A complete stranger arrived one Sunday evening and introduced himself as under-keeper on an estate a few miles away.

He said that he had been instructed to gas a sett and that they had found two starving cubs about a week later. He imagined the old sow had tried to dig her way out from the inside and had been gassed for her courage. Perhaps the boar had opened the sett up, from the outside, and, when the air had circulated and cleared the tunnels, the cubs had been forced, by hunger, into the open, in search of their mother. The young keeper had taken them home, to rear as pets for his children, but one had died.

The other had grown too strong to be imprisoned by ordinary wire netting and the head keeper would not have badgers on the shoot. So, he wondered if it was any good to me.

It was not tame, by any standards, and he needed a pair of thick hedging gloves to get it out of the box. This didn't surprise me because I have often noticed that ferrets kept by keepers are anything but quiet to handle. Many keepers are unimaginative men, who believe that all they need to do is to feed an animal once a day and that its sense of gratitude will make it evermore docile and affectionate.

Its temper didn't matter to me because I had no intention of keeping another tame badger after ten years with Bloody Bill Brock. So I accepted the cub and told the keeper that I should try to establish it at liberty in the wood. For the moment, I put it in a brick-built dog kennel, from which there was no way of escape.

Next morning I hauled a large packing case into position six feet from the mound we'd made from the old tree roots.

I built an exercise run on to it, made from stout steel mesh, enclosing all sides, including the base. The end of this run was right against the butt of one of the tree roots.

My new cub was a little bigger than a cat and excessively nervous of any approach. This was fine, because one of the hazards in liberating hand-reared animals is that, when they have lost their fear of Man, they are abnormally bold about attacking domestic stock.

I felt that, once this little badger did escape into the wood, it would be so delighted that it would take no risk of recapture by venturing near human beings again.

The packing case was only intended as a temporary run and, as soon as it was ready, I introduced the cub.

It was so terrified, when I tried to pick it up, that I put a box filled with straw on the floor of the kennel. With the misguided faith of an ostrich burying his head in sand, the cub dived to the bottom of the box for cover and stayed buried in its false sense of security, until I had transferred it to the pen I had built in the wood.

My purpose in making such a small pen was simply to accustom the inmate to new surroundings. If I had liberated it straight away, I was certain that it would have wandered aimlessly off, and probably gone on wandering till it met someone less kindly disposed to badgers than I am.

In any case it was neither old nor experienced enough to have much chance of survival if it suddenly had to fend for itself.

I fed and watered it in that pen for the next fourteen days. By that time it was so at home that it came out to feed almost as soon as I had gone and I could stay twenty yards down wind and watch quite easily.

The next stage was to cut a hole in the steel mesh, at the end of the run, large enough for it to creep through and escape. I was careful not to make that as easy as it sounds.

I chose the site for the hole so that the only way of escape was to dig a tunnel *into* the earth mound which covered the tree-root sett.

Once inside, I reckoned it would be able to move about freely but would still not be able to escape into the open wood until it had dug another tunnel from the centre to the world outside. By that time, I hoped, it would regard the sett as home and take up permanent quarters there.

The whole process took a surprisingly long time. In the meantime I put food and water in the pen and the cub came back through the hole I'd cut in the steel mesh every night to feed. But it never slept in the packing case after it had dug into the pile of roots.

Each morning I looked carefully round the earth mound to see how long it would be before an escape tunnel appeared.

The first sign was fourteen days after I had cut a way out of the pen. There was now nothing to stop the cub going as far as it liked and, to make sure that food was

My hunch that badgers are not very lethal is strengthened by the reactions of the ducks themselves. Ducks always seem to me to be more intelligent than most birds and are extremely perceptive to danger and safety and who they can trust.

There is a lot of duck shooting in my area and the local syndicate tip whole bags of corn in their flight ponds. Then, when the ducks are feeding freely, they line the banks with guns and fill the evening air with lead.

It is devastating fire power, from which there seems little chance to escape, and I feared that my tame duck would be the first to sacrifice themselves on this 'sporting' altar.

Yet I finish the season with more duck than there were at the beginning. Wild birds join the tame and, whatever the perils of local sporting guns, they quickly acquire the confidence that we don't offer food for six days, here, and shoot our guests the seventh.

Although our own residents are tame, I am certain that they eke out the rations I provide by visiting the perilous pools of my neighbours, because I often see them flighting home at dawn.

When I know a shooting party is due, I give ours double rations, in the hope that they won't stray into danger that night, and they seem to keep out of harm's way so long as they are not pierced by the pangs of hunger.

It is relevant to examine the attitude of wild duck when they are confronted by a badger.

Ours take very little notice of the dogs and are more curious than alarmed by them. But they take to the wing at once if a cat runs along the outside of the fence and are even more scary if they see a fox.

So I often feed them on summer nights in the strip of paddock between the dog kennel and the badger sett.

Bill comes out well before dusk, and at that time the flock of duck is still dibbling for grain in the grass when he appears.

They stop feeding and raise their heads, to be certain what it is, and, if he approaches too near, say within twelve feet, those within range will fly to the far side of the flock. But they show none of the instinctive fear they would exhibit in the presence of foxes or cats.

This would be surprising if badgers were really as destructive as their enemies would have us believe, because ducks are so responsive to peril.

Our own flock demonstrate this not only with dogs and strangers. They will come off the pool and up the paddock if I am carrying a bucket that they expect to be full of corn. But if I walk down with a spade under my arm, which looks like a gun, they take flight as if they had never seen me before.

There is always a proportion of wild ones among them, usually including a few 'limpers' which have escaped, peppered with shot from duck shoots on flight ponds in the district.

Even these are unlikely to have had a good, hard look at a shooting man, because most duck shooting is done as dusk is falling. The first indication they normally have is the searing pain from the shot that cripples them, which would surely be no time for making mental notes that men plus guns equate to agony.

The fact remains that our whole flock is uneasy if I am carrying something of an unusual shape or if they see a strange dog, cat, stoat or fox.

They are quick to assess these signs of potential danger but take little more notice of badgers than the roe deer, just keeping the minimum distance that prudence dictates.

The badger, for his part, seems aware of their superior mobility and does not dissipate his energies by trying to harm them.

My only worry was what would happen on frosty nights, when the ice on the pool was thick enough to bear the weight of Brock.

Our pool is filled mainly by drainage from the wood and would freeze right over if it was not for the ducks, which spend most of the night floating safe on the water and would obviously be far more vulnerable to predation if forced to roost on dry land.

So they take it in turns to swim in circles and prevent the patch of water in the centre from freezing.

They choose different parts of the pool, depending on wind direction and the volume of water draining from the wood, and seem to congregate on the last patch to freeze because it is therefore the easiest to keep ice free.

The harder the weather, the smaller this patch becomes, so I go out each morning to assist by breaking a few extra square yards to ease their efforts.

This is necessary because, when duck cannot keep free water in their chosen pool, they normally fly to the nearest river or estuary. My few pinioned duck can't fly, so it is vital to keep a free patch big enough to attract the rest, which keep swimming round to help them.

Even so, this open patch often shrinks to a few square yards diameter, and I was afraid the badger would creep to the edge and panic the full-winged duck to flight. The pinioned ducks would have tried to join them and fluttered off across the ice.

Then the badger could have followed them, as he followed the silkie bantam, and captured them when they came to the boundary netting or when they took refuge in a thicket.

But my fears were groundless and I have never yet lost a duck to the badger, even in the hard weather. This may be partly due to the fact that badgers are less active when the weather is cold, but the fact remains that they do less harm than even their friends expect.

CHAPTER SIX

No Room in the Wood

Bill was now just on twelve months old and had spent the winter fastened in the enclosure because of the risks of carrying foot-and-mouth disease.

When I had to fasten him in, I hoped he would ease the boredom by enlarging his sett from the drain pipe I'd sunk in the corner of his kennel.

It didn't work out that way. Although badgers are such cleanly creatures, he decided it would make a perfect latrine and I didn't discover his error till he'd almost filled it. There was nothing for it but to dig out the pipe and a few feet of sodden earth around it, refill with clean earth and patch the corner of the box to make it into a kennel with only one entrance.

Had I stopped to consider the standard construction of an artificial fox earth, I shouldn't have made the mistake originally, because sportsmen often have so much more accumulated experience than naturalists. Not only are they careful about the ventilation of the earths they make, but they are also particular to build the roof low enough to make it difficult for the fox to leave his dung, which he normally does in a squatting position.

I was perfectly aware of this but, being brought up on stories of how fastidious badgers are, it never occurred to me that mine would be keen on indoor sanitation. Once I'd made his kennel good and sweetened the earth beneath it, he never transgressed again.

By the end of February, I became aware of another unexpected defect in badgers' characters. Strong badger tracks began to appear along the whole length of the boundary fence, not only inside but outside as well. It was obvious that the wild badgers were visiting him and that he was equally interested in them.

I was delighted about this because I'd always felt guilty, since I had been unable to obtain a young sow, that he really had no more companionship of his own kind than my first one had.

He had acquired some degree of fixation on me, showing an unnaturally intense affection, and he was always more interested in calling at the house for human company than in going about more normal business.

So I decided that, as soon as the danger of foot-and-mouth disease was past, I would throw open the double badger gate again and let him resume the freedom of the outside world and seek the companionship of the wild badgers.

The prospect of watching him shed off his affinities with Man and gradually revert to the wild was very exciting. I couldn't help wondering if he would be prepared to bite the hand that fed him as quickly as his so-called civilized superiors seem to be.

The first indication that his nature was not sweet to its dregs came within a few days. When I went to examine his sett in the morning, to check that all was well, I noticed that he had a nasty gash in his muzzle, extending to his nose. It made no difference to his reception of me, because he whickered his affection as usual and did no worse than chatter with pain, or as a warning, when I held his head to examine the extent of his wound.

It was only a superficial cut, of no grave significance, but it must have been inflicted by a wild badger through the wire-net boundary fence, since Bill was fastened inside.

Wire netting is dreadful stuff to separate two animals which want to fight. If either gets a grip on the other, through the netting, it is only natural for the victim to flinch away. The netting is too strong to give and there is real danger that the aggressor will shear off his main canine teeth in the process.

I have seen game cocks, in adjacent runs, fight through the netting and inflict far worse harm on each other than if they were fighting naturally – and every dog breeder is only too conscious of the peril.

Luckily the foot-and-mouth disease had by now abated in our area and there was no great danger of spreading infection.

Since Bill was a well-grown yearling boar, there seemed less danger for him looking after himself in the wood than continuing to swap insults through the fence.

I reckoned that, outside the enclosure, he would be on other badgers' territory, but that he could retreat to us if he got better than he gave.

Right triumphs in Nature more often than it does with us. An animal on its own territory usually wins, but, in any case, it rarely fights to the death. When one realizes that he has more than met his match, he seeks safety in flight and is normally allowed to escape.

So I expected Bill to get a hiding or two but to deem valour the better part of discretion and bolt for home when he had had enough.

Once through the boundary fence, he would be on his own territory, with Right on his side.

I wasn't very worried that a wild boar would risk coming through anything so trap-like as the double badger gate, but, even if he did, he would be on Bill's territory and have less heart for the battle.

Bill could then 'see him off' and gradually enlarge his

territory by taking more and more outside the gate, as he grew strong and skilful enough to defend it. As the nearest wild sett was several hundred yards away (the sett I keep stunk out), the land round the enclosure would become progressively tainted with Bill's mark.

The fence had been erected for five years, during which time no wild badger had entered, though they were able to get completely round the perimeter. But no wild ones had ever 'owned' it, so that Bill had a very solid claim because his area must be foreign to all others.

So I took him for a few walks in the wood, to refresh his memory of the topography, and to make certain he knew the quickest way home in case of trouble.

Animals have remarkable memories for places and I have seen lurchers go straight to a tussock, that last time held a hare, even if they have not been back for twelve months or more.

I knew at once, from the way Bill started to forage in the undergrowth, instead of staying glued to my heels, that he was not afraid of getting lost.

So I stole quietly away and left him and, when he noticed my absence, he ambled back through the badger gate as if he had done it every night of winter.

Having satisfied myself that he knew how to escape if there was a crisis, I fastened the bolt back and left the badger gate so that he was imprisoned no longer.

I put a straw across the opening so that, when the door swung, it bent or broke the straw so that I could see when he had been out.

I knew quite well that he might find another sett, or even dig one for himself, which would be more attractive than mine. I knew, too, that he was very likely to take up with a sow badger and forget me, at best, or even take a dislike, as wild badgers understandably dislike the human race.

In theory, this shouldn't disturb me, because my declared object had been to see how long a hand-reared badger would remain tame when offered complete freedom. I had vowed never to keep another captive.

When it came to the crunch, I hoped he wouldn't go. I hoped, instead, that he would bring a bride home to the sett I had made. It would have affronted my pride if he had bitten me after all the affection he had shown.

Each morning, I examined the badger gate, to see if he had been out. When he had, I went to his sett, ostensibly to make sure he was back, but subconsciously, perhaps, to reassure myself that his affection was not abating.

It was not many mornings before all was not well. I knew something was amiss, long before I had crossed the paddock to check the badger gate into the wood.

As soon as I went out to feed the ducks, Mandy, the oldest lurcher, feathered as if a hare had just passed, and hunted the line swiftly and surely to the entrance to the sett.

I knew it wasn't a hare, because hares can't get into the paddock, and the tunnel to a badger sett would not have been its idea of a safe haven for the day, if it had.

I didn't think it was Bill because the dogs have known him all his life and do not take the slightest notice either of him or the trail he leaves, because the whole paddock must reek of his scent every morning of the year.

Wondering if a fox had, after all, braved the double gate or if a wild badger had joined him already, I hurried across to his sett to check.

I found a sizeable pool of blood on the stone slab at

the mouth of his tunnel, so it was evidently the blood that had excited the dogs.

When I opened the sett, Bill was there all right, with quite a tough neck injury and a large hole punctured in his foot, which had evidently dripped blood across the paddock.

The original gash on his face had completely healed, and I was naturally rather perturbed by this new evidence of pugnacity. As the wounds were only superficial, and badgers make bad patients, I decided to leave him to heal them himself.

When I got through the gate into the wood, the dogs became excited again and hunted up and down the open ride, before striking a line through the wood, and across the open fields to the sett the wild badgers used.

Following more slowly behind, I was delighted to see small pools of blood tracing the path the badger had taken.

It did occur to me that Bill might have ventured too far and that this trail was perhaps left by him when he retreated for home.

If this was so, the dogs were hunting 'heel', in the reverse direction to that taken by their quarry.

When I got to the wild badgers' sett, there were footprints much larger than Bill's, and the dogs had a more menacing note than they ever use to him, so I was pretty certain that this was his adversary.

Judging by the amount of blood, Bill had given quite as good as he got, so I felt more satisfied and very proud of him.

My pride seemed justified when nothing else happened for the next ten days.

The straw across the badger gate was broken each morning, and Bill was safely back and asleep by the time

I went to check that all was well. Perhaps the battle he'd fought had settled the boundaries for both territories and he had now acquired part of the wood outside where he could go with impunity.

All went well for about a fortnight and then I noticed padding each side of the fence again.

Last time I had assumed that they had not been bluffing but had genuinely been trying to get at each other. But, if it was a rough house they wanted, there was now nothing to stop either going through the badger gate to get at the other. The straw was broken next morning to indicate that both had been in the same part of the wood, though not necessarily at the same time.

Perhaps this was psychological warfare. Perhaps each marched up and down 'his' side of the netting, like Red Indians at a war dance, or Great Powers conducting army manoeuvres near each other's frontier.

The net result seemed to be the same. When such a flood of insults had poured out from each side that neither could stomach them a moment longer, they sallied forth to battle.

It was difficult to tell how seriously they took it because, once more, Bill's wounds were not serious. They were nasty, painful, but superficial for all that. This time, the worst was a savage bite through the ham of his near hind leg.

I was none too happy about these recurrent fights because, though he was very well grown for a yearling boar, he was by no means fully mature. Combined with the fact that he was hand reared, and still having artificial food, I feared his physical condition could not be as sharp as a fully wild boar that had always had to fend for himself.

At the end of March, I acquired two sow cubs, at the

right age to hand rear, though I did not intend that they should grow up as tame as Bill.

I put them in the dog kennel, next door to where I had reared Bill, and fed him outside, where he could see, hear and smell, but could not touch them.

If I reared them successfully, which ought to be easy, and if he took to them, which might be more difficult to arrange, they ought to solve the problem of his loneliness.

The third and most important 'if' was if he was still alive by the time they grew up.

I was bottle-feeding the cubs first thing in the morning, last thing at night and twice in between. All had been well for three weeks after Bill's last skirmish, and I was lulled once more into a false sense of security.

On the third of May, we were out very late at a party, returning at a quarter to one in the morning.

I gave the young badgers their bottle and went to feed the dogs. Normally, they sit in a respectful semi-circle, watching me cut up their meat with eager anticipation. That night they were nowhere to be seen.

When I went to see where they were, I found them dancing up and down the boundary fence, obviously itching to get into the wood.

I imagined a fox was somewhere near, but made them lie down so that I could listen for myself.

From a long way up the wood, a faint, unmistakable sound drifted through the trees. It was badgers screaming in fury or agony, I knew not which. Even then, I was more curious than worried.

I went to the house for a torch, shut the dogs in the study and set off up the wood. I went quietly and, though there was not much moon, I used my torch as little as possible, but there was no doubt which direction the screams were coming from.

The chattering climbed to a crescendo when I got to a clearing, about four hundred yards from the house, and above the screams, a laboured, moaning breathing was all too obvious.

I switched on the torch and could see two grey forms, writhing on the ground, the top one shaking and worrying, like a fighting bull terrier.

They didn't break it up till I was within about five yards, and then the one which had clearly been winning, stopped tearing his opponent and disappeared into the shadows.

The other didn't move. He lay, flat on his belly, filling the air with stertorous wheezes.

He was utterly exhausted.

Shining the torch on him, there was no doubt that it was my Bill Brock, so I gave him a few minutes to recover his breath.

Although he was so wonderfully tame, I did not fancy touching him in such distress, lest he be still trigger-happy enough to grab anything which came near.

It would not even be safe to touch a favourite dog so soon after such a hiding, and Bill was clearly so sore that it would be difficult to touch a spot which wasn't excruciatingly painful. So I waited till he recovered sufficiently to follow me home, so that I could bolt his badger gate and leave him shut in safety in the paddock.

I underestimated his injuries. If I'd waited an hour, he would still not have been fit to stagger home by himself. So, probably foolishly, I plucked up courage to pick him up.

He made not the slightest attempt to bite me, nor did he give his usual affection call. The only sound he made was a faint chatter, to show how unbearable his agony was, and then he lay limp in my arms.

I carried him home to the lighted yard, so that I could examine his injuries, and put him down by a bowl of water. The only movement he made was the laboured heaving of his flanks, as he gasped for breath.

After a time, he took a few gulps of water and, as the only damage I could see was a series of wounds at the back of his neck, I carried him to the mouth of his sett.

He struggled out of sight, up the pipe, not walking but dragging himself, by his forelegs, almost as if he'd broken his back.

Next morning, I went out at first light, not knowing what to expect. When I lifted the lid of his kennel, I found him completely covered with bedding, but he poked out his head and whickered a faint welcome.

I ran my hands over him, to assess the damage, but he was so very tender that he chattered with pain and I decided not to worry him.

I fetched a bowl of water, from which he had a few sips, but he was not in the least interested in food. I couldn't even tempt him with raw egg or pure honey.

That night, he took a little more water, but it was not till next day that I discovered the full extent of the mischief.

When I went next morning, I scraped away the bedding which still covered him and gently rolled him over. He protested feebly, but made no attempt to bite me.

The back of his neck was moderately lacerated, there was a gash on his muzzle and another on his nearside shoulder.

The real damage was to his hindquarters. His opponent had gripped him by the base of his tail, where it joins the main spinal column, and literally skinned it.

With this as the focal point of his attack, he had pulped the whole hindquarters, which were beginning to scab over by the time I examined them.

Perhaps this was the reason why Bill had apparently done so little to defend himself, because he had been stretched out prone, when I found him, taking all the punishment his opponent dished out.

The mode of attack reminded me of a party trick, performed in pubs by an old professional rat catcher I once knew.

This old man used to pick up a rat by the end of its tail and hold it dangling, head down. As anyone who has ever tried to pick a rat up by its tail will know the animal's reaction is to double up and climb up its own tail till it can bite the hand which holds it.

The old rat catcher would allow the rat to approach to within an inch of his thumb and finger and then cry 'Down, Boy,' whereupon the rat would seem to heed the command, straighten its back, and hang motionless, head down again.

The performance would be repeated as often as anyone was willing to buy another drink, but the rat's reactions were not a matter of training.

As long as it was held between the ball of the old man's thumb and his finger, it could climb up to defend itself. But pinching its tail between his horny nails appeared to have an almost paralytic effect on the animal, which stretched out straight as if by reflex action.

I wonder if badgers do the same thing. I wonder if, by gripping the tail between such powerful jaws, it forces the victim to stretch out, either in unbearable agony or because the nerves of the spine are involuntarily activated.

Shrews will sometimes fight by similar methods and I have watched them deliberately trying to bite each other's tail.

Whatever the explanation of the theory of such attack,

the result was that Bill Brock was very ill indeed. I discussed the symptoms with my vet, but badgers are not easy creatures for strangers to treat with anaesthetics, and we decided, since it was an area he could lick, that, on balance, he would treat it better himself.

He might have struggled and done himself more harm if we had messed him about.

I continued to visit him with food and water twice a day and, though he was always grateful for the water, he did not touch a morsel of food for eight full days.

I didn't press him because, for that time, he never emptied himself properly, because his hind parts must have been so excruciating.

Nor, so far as I could tell, did he come out of his sett during that time, but, on the ninth morning, the sett was empty when I went to visit him.

I took this as a good sign and found that he had returned to the dog kennel where he was reared, and was lying-up in a box of straw there. Luckily, I had moved the two little sow cubs to the room next door, because it was easier to fit the infra-red lamp there, so his old place was vacant.

Although I was pleased, at first, that Bill was showing signs of mobility, I was puzzled about the reason.

That night, or at two o'clock in the morning to be precise, we found out.

We were awakened by the clattering of the iron wicket gate below our bedroom window, which connects the garden to the paddock.

It is the only way into the garden from the paddock, except up the ha-ha wall, and Bill tries it every night to see if we have forgotten to fasten it.

If we have, he is through like a shot, and a very bad

gardener he is, because he always chooses my wife's most cherished bulbs, or the most vulnerable patch of lawn, in which to dig a hole.

The garden itself is still within the boundary fence, so that he has to return the same way.

The gate was firmly closed, that night, so we were delighted to hear the furious rattling probing through our slumber. Bill could not be as bad as I thought if he was up to such old tricks again.

By this time the moon was full and it was a glorious night, so I got out of bed to see what he was up to.

I leaned half-way out of the window and was astonished to discover that he was not in the paddock, trying to get into the garden, as I'd thought. He was in the garden, trying to get into the paddock.

I called down to him, to see what he was at – and there was a startled snort and he was gone.

It took a few seconds to dawn on me that it hadn't been Bill at all. It must have been his rival.

I pulled on a pair of trousers and jacket and went down to the dog kennel to check that all was well with Bill.

I found him cowering in the back of his box, obviously terrified.

I reached for a rifle and torch and let Tough, the alsatian, out into the garden. She feathered at once, obviously excited that a stranger had been on her territory. Then she marked by the garden gate and I could see where our visitor had dug a hole under the netting and entered from outside. I reckoned he wouldn't risk another visit that night, stuck a rock in the hole, and went back to bed.

Next morning, I examined the whole boundary fence,

foot by foot. It is a thousand yards long and there were several patches where the wild boar had tested it from outside, found it impregnable, and passed on. The places where he'd scratched were obvious.

The whole footing of the fence is either buried or fastened to concrete, and it has a strand of barbed wire stretched, taut, along the bottom of the netting, to make it almost impossible to dig through.

In the whole of that thousand yards, there was only one single yard not so treated.

I remembered, when we put up the fence, that we had run out of barbed wire at the very last spot, but had not worried because we did not think wild things would come so near the house and, if they did, they would only get as far as the garden. To get out of the paddock, it was necessary to pass the ha-ha first.

That wild boar had evidently tried every foot of the fence until he came to that one, weak spot.

He had forced an entry and was trying to break through the wicket gate, which is the second line of defence, when we had wakened up.

He could, of course, have dropped down, from the lawn, over the ha-ha, which is only four foot six deep, but presumably, he knew that he couldn't get back if he did, since badgers are no jumpers and exceptionally poor climbers. So he hadn't let his heart run away with his head!

There was only one attraction inside that fence. Bill Brock. There is no doubt in my mind that that wild boar had murder in his heart and that he meant to finish the job which I had interrupted a week before.

Bill's own actions strengthened the theory. He loved his sett and had never slept a day away from it since he found it as a cub. Yet something had prompted him to leave it the moment his injuries allowed him to struggle so far.

The sett is within ten yards of the boundary fence, so Bill, lying there in his painful misery, must have heard his conqueror trying to break in within a few yards of where he convalesced.

He would have smelt him, too, and know that the additional stench from his own wounds must have betrayed his hiding place.

So he moved to the building which, in addition to the sow cubs, also housed the dogs, which were free to roam in the night. Not the most attractive place for even the most vindictive wild badger to follow.

The conclusion I draw, from all this, is that, if I had not arrived in time, I am certain in my own mind that the wild boar would have killed Bill Brock. He had got him completely defenceless and was so intent on destruction that he allowed me to approach within five yards before breaking off the engagement.

I am by no means convinced by the theory that wild animals disputing territory do not fight to the death, holds water.

This view is strengthened by the fact that the wild boar was prepared to go to such lengths to follow his partial victory up, a week later, even to the extent of entering what must certainly be regarded as Bill's territory.

Keeping in mind that a pair of badgers can have three or four cubs a year, and that their life span could be in excess of ten years, it is obvious that, in theory, the badger population might increase much more than, in fact, it does.

Their major enemy is Man, who is growing more tolerant towards them than he was, yet their numbers have not increased as dramatically as theory might postulate. What, then, maintains the population in relative balance?

It could be that badgers are susceptible to some disease, as weasels are prone to parasitic worms, which enter their sinus and attack their skulls. It could be that, like foxes, they suffer from distemper or jaundice. But I know of no evidence to substantiate the idea.

I wonder if badgers are not, perhaps, the worst enemy of other badgers? I wonder if cubs, driven from the parental sett, do not always settle as easily as supposed, elsewhere, but are sometimes exterminated, not by fools with dogs or gas, but by other badgers?

I do not postulate this as a theory because one isolated instance means no more than a swallow makes a summer. But I offer the suggestion as food for further thought and, perhaps, as a suggestion for further research.

If there is proved to be much in it, then it will be one more strong reason why people should be discouraged from rearing badger cubs, because it means that they must fret in captivity or be subject to unknown hazards if their owners tire of them and set them free. Based on my experience with Bill, it is tantamount to a particularly unpleasant death sentence.

I have recounted this to various people who have kept badgers and found several other instances where wild badgers have tried, with varying degrees of success, to break into the captive's cage, sometimes with fatal results.

It has, of course, been suggested that Bill is a tame badger, tainted with the stench of Man.

The suggestion is that wild badgers will not tolerate him for this reason and that it is not so much that he is on their territory that they object to, as the fact that he has an unnatural affinity with their enemy.

I do not hold with this because experiments have been tried where badgers, dug out for sport by badger diggers, have been turned down to improve the stock elsewhere. Even when they have been marked with conspicuous dyes, they have rarely been seen again.

They may, of course, have wandered, and a stranger seeing a red, white or blue badger may have kept it under his hat lest friends cast doubt on his sobriety.

Apart from road casualties, it is almost as rare to find a dead badger in the open as a dead donkey. But badgers are tough creatures and, half paralysed as he was, Bill did manage to crawl into his sett and, even if his adversary had mauled him worse, I believe he would have made the supreme effort to die in his own bed or, at least, shuffled out of sight in cover.

If he had died in his sett, he would have rotted to a skeleton and, eventually, his bones would have been brought to the surface by subsequent generations.

Every badger digger knows that bones of badgers, long since dead and gone, often turn up in the soil and bedding in the mound outside the sett.

They could be badgers which have died cubbing or of disease or old age. Or they could have been gassed, deliberately or in mistake for foxes or rabbits.

But it is not impossible that some of them are the remains of badgers killed by their own kind.

Whether Bill Brock had been attacked because he was in another badger's territory or because he was tainted with Man, made little difference to me.

The fact remained that he had been attacked with murderous intent and that an attempt had been made to finish the job.

It seemed to me inevitable that he would be attacked again and that, perhaps next time, I wouldn't be on hand to rescue him.

If only for the purely practical and selfish reason that I had put a great deal of effort into rearing and taming him, I was anxious to avoid this. But, far more important, we had developed a genuine bond of mutual affection and I was just as loth to see him hurt as I should have been if he was a favourite dog. So I prepared to go to almost any lengths to prevent him getting another such hiding.

The simple fact emerged that if Bill was not to die, his attacker must. So I took a rifle, at dawn, and went to the sett where I was certain he lived, and waited quietly to perform his execution.

Normally, I can see the badgers at this sett more or less at will, but I waited for dawns and I waited for dusks and I never got a shot. So I did what I should have done at first, and stank out the sett with Reynardine.

Bill was gradually recovering, but I kept him shut in the enclosure. I persuaded myself that I wanted to do some work on the time of year when badgers are most aggressive.

The simple way seemed to be to record the periods when Bill and his adversaries showed mutual animosity through the netting.

It would have the attractive fringe benefit of preventing him being killed!

Nothing happened for a long time after he recovered. It was summer and food was plenteous and the irregular six-acre enclosure disguised the fact that he was really caged in.

At the end of June, a strange badger started digging latrine pits on the other side of the netting, a sure indication that he was staking a territorial claim.

I visited the wild sett and found that the reek of Reynardine had apparently worn off, because it had been opened up again.

So I gave it another dose, which seemed to drive the invader far enough away to make our place unattractive again.

By now, Bill was not only adult but reaching full maturity. He was a fine, husky young boar who looked good enough for anything.

All went well until the night of August 28th. We were awakened at a quarter to two in the morning by the dreaded chattering of fighting badgers.

This time it wasn't four hundred yards away, but more like forty, in the centre of the paddock between the house and the pool.

I wasted no time but grabbed a rifle and a torch and rushed out clothed as I was. I could see them at it, as before, but daren't shoot because it was impossible to distinguish which was which.

Last time they could have been fighting for an hour, for all I knew, but, this time I was certain that they had roused us out of slumber almost as soon as they started.

They broke up when I got to within about ten yards, Bill seeming pleased and coming to greet me and his opponent dashing off round the far side of the pool.

My wife, who had a dress circle seat in the bedroom window, could hear the wild boar gasping for breath, as Bill had done last time. He was so distressed that she could plot his progress by ear, right round the far side of the pool, more than two hundred yards from the house.

Meanwhile, I'd gone back to fetch Tough and laid her on his line. I hoped she would bring him to bay so that I could terminate his career.

She hunted him right round the pool and back towards the house, into a thicket on the north side of the paddock.

Unfortunately I had to call her off, here, because I knew my roe deer was lying-up in that area, with a bad eye I was dressing daily with antibiotics.

Although she is perfectly used to Tough, I feared that a sudden commotion might panic her and make her blunder into some obstacle and aggravate the damage to her eye.

So I had to leave him, and next morning he had dug his way to freedom under the fence where it was not buried as deeply as it should have been because it passed over a tree root.

When I searched to find where he had entered, I discovered that he had bitten through the one stretch of light-gauge netting in the whole perimeter fence. He certainly was adept at probing for weak spots because, to the best of my knowledge, he had ferreted out the only two there were in the whole fence.

I did not know whether Bill had developed enough extra strength to master him or whether it was not the same boar that had given him his original thrashing, but the symptoms of distress that he exhibited were exactly similar to the ones I'd heard Bill make, and we have not been troubled by him since.

I was naturally very wary about letting Bill out again and I make a daily inspection of the boundary fence, to see if there is any sign of fresh latrine pits to indicate that strangers are about.

I also visit the sett on my neighbour's farm at least once a week to check that no holes had been opened up.

If they have, I simply stink it out again so that our area can only come on the edge of other territory instead of in the middle. It seems that we are not troubled until badgers have occupied the area for long enough to regard it as 'theirs' and regular stinking seems to be what is required to keep interlopers on the move.

Meanwhile, Bill is developing towards his prime, so that he is no longer easy meat, as the intruder who got into the paddock discovered.

I have obviously interfered with the natural pattern of this aggression by turning the intruders out of their sett with Reynardine, so it is impossible to be definitive about its cause or the seasons when it is most likely to occur.

The first real trouble we had was when wild cubs would just about be venturing from their sett.

So the first attacks might have been as a preventative against ours attacking their cubs, though I have no evidence that the cubs would be in any danger.

The second time, in August, would be after the rut, when one would expect boars to be spent and disinclined for war.

Wild badgers appear to work our boundary fence soon after they have settled in a neighbouring sett and the time of year seems less important than the distance from the nearest inhabited colony.

The trouble ceases as soon as they are stunk out, so my theory is that our land is traditionally associated with the territory attached to that sett.

So I shall try to keep it regularly stunk out until a new generation of wild badgers has grown up, which has never regarded it as 'home'.

By the time, perhaps, Bill will have founded a colony of our own here and have right on his side when he goes to warn off any youngsters who dare to intrude in our wood. The long-term strategy seems to be to try to shift the seat of power from the wild sett, in the valley, to our artificial setts here. International politicians might have much to learn from a study of neighbouring colonies of badgers.

CHAPTER SEVEN

Les Girls

My naturalist friends, hearing my stories of gory aggression, sowed seeds of doubt about my ability to introduce Bill to the cubs without loss of life. 'As soon as he found them in his territory,' they said, 'he would almost certainly savage them.'

It needed no such pessimism to shake my confidence, but I comforted myself with the hope that badgers couldn't really be such misogamists or their whole race would fizzle out. But it did get me a little worried when I saw how Bill was treated by other members of his race and how he, in turn, bore bottomless grudges against them.

Having a practical nature, I decided to rear not one but two. When the time came to introduce them to the boar, I would try one first and keep the other for hard lines.

Then, if he killed the first, I would keep the other until she was sexually mature and came in season. There's nothing like a taste of sex to change a man's mind about women!

There was many a bridge to cross before that. When they arrived, these cubs had just been dug out and introduced to the bottle.

The infra-red lamp, I had used to rear Bill, was still set up to supply their warmth, and I had found it much better than the old electric bulb in a tin. It had the great advantage of being easily adjusted for intensity of heat, because all that was necessary was to raise or lower it a little.

When the time came to wean the cubs off artificial heat, I could do it gradually simply by raising the source a few inches a day.

Bill had been reared on a towel, stretched over the floor of his sleeping box, which had been an ideal arrangement because it was almost clinically clean, could be replaced daily, and I could see at a glance if he had emptied himself and if his motions were satisfactory.

I have had considerable experience at rearing all sorts of wild creatures and cannot conceive what induced me to depart from this well-tried routine.

Perhaps it was because, when the sow cubs arrived, they looked so comfortable in a box of straw. Whatever the reason, the fact remains that, instead of bedding them on stretched towel, I used soft oat straw.

This added to the difficulty of ascertaining that their motions were correct and I cannot over-emphasize that there is nothing which will cause young things to fade and die so surely as dehydration, caused by loss of moisture, or a stoppage caused by constipation.

The trouble was doubled by having two cubs together because it was impossible to assess which symptoms belonged to which, and I had to treat both for any irregularity suspected in either.

But badgers are tough and, apart from the odd nasty moment, both thrived and grew well.

Then I noticed that, instead of their coats thickening up and growing darker, the hairs seems to get sparse and spiky as hedgehogs, and there were obvious signs of intense irritation, because they backed repeatedly round the box, rubbing themselves on the floor and chattering loudly.

The long-suffering vet, whose signature tune was, by now, to the effect that he had little experience with badgers, was of the opinion that the trouble was caused by dietary deficiency.

They had been started on human baby food, instead of the Lactol that I preferred, and it was obvious that it may have lacked something badger sow's milk had.

So we tried adding vitamin concentrates to each feed, although the cubs were fat and growing well, but their coats continued to deteriorate steadily and, worse still, one eye of each cub discoloured to a horrible, sinister blue.

The real cause of the trouble only dawned on me in the nick of time. One dreadful morning, I noticed that both cubs had a most unpleasant, husky rattle in their breathing.

I had asked both the vet and a doctor friend if the skin trouble could be some form of dermatitis, but the symptoms were, apparently, not right.

When I heard the breathing, it reminded me at once of the noise pigs make when they have virus pneumonia. And virus pneumonia can be induced in pigs by allowing them to breathe fine dust.

My poor little badger cubs were certainly breathing that. The drying heat from the infra-red lamps was desiccating the straw until the least movement would crumble it to a friable dust which must have been a frightful irritant.

It had got in their eyes, it had fetched off their hair and, at last, it had affected their breathing.

We were lucky to discover the cause just in time and we replaced the straw with a soft clean towel. For the next four weeks, I treated them with penicillin eye ointment and massaged their almost bare little bodies with olive oil after each feed.

I normally love to show my friends any creature that is sharing our home and take pride in demonstrating their shining health and the fact that they live full and happy lives.

But when anyone wanted to see these two little sows, I hung my head in shame. They did me no credit at all, and I was conscious that their discomfort was due to my crass stupidity.

My cure for personal worry is to pause and think what I was worried about exactly a year ago to the day. The fact that it is usually quite difficult to remember, cuts the present trouble down to size.

'A year from now,' I think, 'this will have shrunk in perspective until I shall have to cudgel my brain to pinpoint it.'

As I write this, it is almost exactly a year since the fact that I had caused considerable discomfort to two innocent cubs amounted almost to a guilt complex.

Today, they are free, adult, sound sighted, with enough coat to make a gross of genuine badger-hair shaving brushes. It is difficult to visualize what scruffy mites they were.

Rearing them together prevented either of them getting a fixation on me, as Bill had done. As they developed, they ate in competition, slept close as lovers, to keep each other warm, and played themselves tired when they were bored.

I had altered the geography of the dog kennel slightly, to accommodate them. The brick shed, which opened directly on to the paddock, was where I had reared Bill.

That had been the coalshed and I still left it so that Bill could get in, though I excluded him from the run. He slept there when the wild boar banished him from his sett by the hawthorn tree.

Next door was the old cottage privy, so I opened that out on to the run and reared the sows in there.

When the weather was fine, they could come into the run, but I shut them up in wet weather because their coats were not yet recovered. I also shut them in at night, just in case Bill chewed through the netting to get at them.

Once the initial problems caused by wrong bedding had been overcome, the main problem was how – and when – to introduce them to Bill.

The fact that only wire netting separated them from the paddock, where the boar roamed every night, meant that he could not avoid their scent, which must have soon lost its novelty.

This was not necessarily very significant because the same had applied to his enemy the wild boar.

In that case each had fumed along his side of the fence, digging dung pits on the very boundary to express his opinion of the other and to stake his claim of tenure.

Each must have inhaled the other's infuriating odour and, far from growing accustomed to it, they had been overwhelmed with mutual fury.

So I didn't lay too much store by the fact that Bill nightly might be inspired by the fragrance of the brides I proposed for him. He had yet to exhibit any desire for matrimony.

To satisfy my curiosity, I went to the run every night to play with the cubs and, when he came out, I called him to the netting.

He always came, because of our mutual affection, and the cubs came too. They all showed every sign of supreme indifference, and Bill made no sign at all that he was even aware that they were there.

The next step, as they grew older and more active, was to take them into the paddock to play, before the old boar was about.

All young things at play are delightful and these cubs were especially so. They fluffed out their fur, which was now growing nicely, and rocked about like bucking broncos. They rolled each other over and over and, when the game grew too unladylike and rough, they chattered with ill-bred temper.

The dogs came too. Not to get them steady with the badgers, because they were already that, but to get the badgers steady with the dogs.

This time, I didn't try to teach them the stretch of territory in front of the house, because I was nervous that they might suddenly get wind of the badger sett and go to ground. I trembled to think what would happen if they appeared, unannounced, in the tunnel and woke Bill up. If he did attack them below ground, there was nothing I could do to help.

I made an entrance from their run to the paddock, through an ordinary six-inch drain pipe. They could easily escape through this but Bill was far too fat and large to follow, so I encouraged them to play in a nightly increasing arc, with this pipe at the centre.

When the time came to let them all free, they could always retreat 'home' through this pipe, and I could also feed them in their run in the certainty that they got what I intended with no chance of the boar scoffing more than his share.

Although Bill disregarded them entirely through the netting, I was wary of letting him meet them face to face, at least until they were agile enough to beat him to the draw in a retreat for home, and too big for him to slay at a single bite.

I took my courage in one, if not both, hands in the third week in May. Up till then, I had let the cubs play nightly, to get the paddock reeking with their taint, but I had always shut them up before the boar appeared. Then I waited to see if he showed any sign of interest when he reached the area of their play.

With considerable misgivings, I kept one out but shut the other safely away. It was like presenting a maiden to a primitive priest. I didn't know if he would fall down and worship her or slap her on his sacrificial altar.

As he approached, my courage nearly failed and I almost scooped her up in a frantic gesture of last-minute rescue. I was too well aware what a murderer I should feel if he mauled her.

He came directly to me, demanding fuss — and I picked him up.

It was a cowardly action but I managed to kid myself that I had only capitulated in order to put him in a good mood before he met the cub.

Any psychologist would have told me I was simply putting off potential trouble; that I was a puny escapist, turning my head away in ostrich-like self deception.

It suited Bill all right. He whickered his delight and revelled in his sensual abandon.

When I could fool myself no longer, I put him down and he played his favourite trick on me. He has never bitten me in malice, but when he doesn't want to be put down, he slides his head under his fore leg — as badgers often do in attack — and grips the hand that carries him. Not viciously, but far too firmly for it to be possible to withdraw it without tearing the flesh.

It is a very skilful exhibition of judgement for, by the time he does deign to release his grip, the pattern of his dentition shows as a depression in the flesh, but never breaks the skin.

If the sensation of pain is any guide, a pennyweight more of pressure would make a bloody wound.

This evening, when my nerves were already frayed with fear for the cub, his craftsmanship excelled itself.

As I bent to put him down, he grasped my hand and held me, doubled up, till the blood rushed to my face. It was small consolation to know that it was not malice but a simple measure of his esteem.

At last he let me go and, before the circulation had returned to my hand, he and the cub had met.

It was an anti-climax. Each showed complete indifference to the other and, though they literally touched, they never even dallied to sniff and neither squatted to stake a claim of possession with his taint.

I lifted the shutter, to let the other cub free from the dog kennel, and the cubs began to play. They romped and rolled and chattered, but still Bill took no notice. Gradually they approached him until they cannoned into him with all the ill manners of youth.

I stood with bated breath. Would his patience pass its peak, or would he show them tolerance?

Almost in slow motion, the old boar began to play. It was a ponderous, self-conscious performance, full of clownish dignity.

The cubs, at first, looked scared, as well they might, but as they realized he meant them no harm, they hotted-up the pace.

Remembering how unintentionally rough my first brock had been, how excruciatingly boisterous, I feared for their safety. But the old boy grew bored and wandered off on one of his nightly forays.

After that, things never looked back. Every night, I let

the cubs out about the time Bill was due to appear from his sett and supervised them for about an hour, but always shut them in safety when I had to go.

No longer in the close confinement of the shed but in the larger liberty of the run, where they could fraternize with Bill whenever they liked during the night, from the safety their side of the netting.

Within a fortnight it was obvious he meant them no harm, at least when their meetings were confined to relatively small doses, so I left them at large till it was time for me to go to bed. Then, just as a precaution, I shut them up.

They gradually ceased to regard the boar solely as a potential playmate. They did play for a few minutes, at first, but when he got bored and went off, they began to follow close behind.

Till then, they had rooted for slugs and insects instinctively but not particularly effectively. When they were with Bill, they waited for him to start rooting and then joined in, nose to nose, when they thought he was on to something good.

They must have been an awful bore, but he was wonderfully patient and, when he did get to the source of his search, he often wandered off and left it to them.

Sooner or later, the novelty flagged and he retreated purposefully, deep into the wood.

This was very effective because the cubs would only follow as far as the territory they knew – and then they'd come back to the kennel.

The most pessimistic observer could not have convinced himself that the old boar nursed any venom in his heart, so, at the end of the first week in June, I ceased to confine the cubs at all, except, of course, within the six-acre enclosure.

The only concession I made to caution was to leave the six-inch pipe as entrance to the run they used in the kennel. If the worst ever did come to the worst, at least they would have somewhere to take refuge.

When I went to feed them on June 19th, they were absent from home and I found them safe with Bill, snuggled in the comfort of his sett.

I had never taken them near it. Either they had found it themselves and he had welcomed them, or they had gone there at his specific invitation.

It gave me a feeling of indescribable satisfaction. After seeing what an indefatigable creature my first Bloody Bill Brock had been, I had always been sensitive of keeping a badger without the company of his own kind.

Circumstances had prevented me from giving Bill the home I'd wanted for more than a year until I'd almost despaired of ever getting him on friendly terms with his own kind.

At last, all three seemed set for a happier and fuller life than is possible for almost any captive badgers.

Knowing that his loneliness was at last over, I believe gave me as much pleasure as him.

It did dawn on me that three badgers at liberty about the place might hardly be an unmixed blessing for the roe deer and duck.

So I decided to do what I could to limit the potential disturbance in their lives.

Having spent my holiday money the previous year on the ha-ha, which had already given us more pleasure than a decade of holidays, I decided this year, that I'd prefer an island in the pool to a fortnight at some expensive hotel.

When the bulldozer came to dredge it out, I was in

bed with flu, so my wife spent a memorable three or four days.

I pushed the bed to the window, where I could watch every spadeful he dug, but, as so often happens, our minds were not in tune. I kept roaring for my wife and asking her to tell him to 'leave that bit' or 'dig that channel a yard wider' or 'get the spoil pile higher, but further off'.

Except for brief 'rests', when she was bringing food and drink and medicine to me, she spent her days dashing up and down the paddock, like a yo-yo, passing messages to the dozer driver which deflated what self confidence he had.

By the time I recovered, the job was done and the pool was a more interesting, kidney shape, with a sizeable island, about ten yards from the bank.

I had a channel, about four yards long and four feet wide, cut from the bank on each side of the pool. My purpose was to fence from the blind end of these channels to the boundary netting. The deer could easily leap over the four feet width, but the badgers would be unable to jump this or climb the netting, and so would not be able to get round the far side of the pool.

So the deer and the duck could have about three acres of reed and bramble and thickets which would be entirely undisturbed by badgers.

The badgers, for their part, could pop through their double badger gate into the wood outside and go wherever they liked, in addition to the paddock and wood inside the perimeter fence near the house. This, of course, is available to them whether the badger gate is bolted or open.

The reason that I thought this would be a practical arrangement is a copybook example of how vital it is not to take theories as viable, simply because they have been passed down from one generation to the next.

I had been brought up on keepers' tales, often repeated in the sporting press and books, that the infallible way to trap badgers is on a fallen tree where they cross ditches and brooks.

'Badgers will never get their feet wet,' this folk tale says. 'They will go for miles up and down a stream to find a dry crossing place.'

They are such clean creatures that I never questioned it and had my channels cut in supreme confidence. It was such a plausible theory.

One lovely warm evening, a few weeks later, I had waded out on to the island to adjust some duck nesting boxes the crows were plagueing.

Looking up, I noticed Bill Brock, working the edge of the pool, testing the air delicately, to see where my scent was coming from.

I couldn't resist calling to him and was amused by his obvious surprise that I appeared to be in the middle of the pool, since I doubt if his eyesight was good enough to distinguish the island.

He walked along the bank till he was directly down-wind, stepped into the water without a moment's hesitation and swam strongly out to me.

He looked even more like a hedgehog when swimming than he does when seen from behind when he was walking, and when he arrived he paid me interest for playing a joke on him. He was delighted as ever to see me and appeared to have enjoyed his bathe.

The shower of water with which he covered me when he shook drenched me so thoroughly that there was no further point in trying to keep dry, so I picked him up in my arms and lavished him with praise for teaching me one more old wives' tale that I could consign to the rubbish tip.

The practical good it served was to save me the physical labour of completing the fence from the channels to the boundary.

One of the fringe benefits of having the island made was a large spoilheap of silt dredged from the pool.

It is a mound about twelve feet high and half as big as a tennis court, directly opposite the sitting-room window and eighty yards away. It was initially very unsightly but the rich silt had grown a restful green covering from a few handfuls of grass seed within a surprisingly few weeks, so that it now reminds me of some megalithic burial place.

Badgers in the wild are reputed to leave their setts at intervals and remove to other quarters. I am not yet convinced that, like so much other badger lore, this is not an over-simplification, because I know of some setts which never seem to be untenanted.

But, if our badgers ever delight us by breeding, it is almost certain that one artificial sett will not be enough.

If Bill proves to be monogamous, another thing about which I remain to be convinced, it is likely that he and whichever sow he chooses will tip the other out. Or the two sows may well throw him out into the cold.

If there is no alternative accommodation, it is probable that whichever has to be odd man out will go off into the wood, where it is much more difficult to observe them in detail.

It seemed to me that, once it has properly drained, this pile of silt from the pool will be wonderfully warm and dry and make the perfect spot for another artificial sett. Although it is further from the window than the other, it is still in full view and quite near enough for every detail to spring to vivid life through a decent pair of binoculars.

We began preparations by digging a deep hole in the centre of the mound and piping a trench to take away any water which percolated through.

Instead of mounting the box on a pile of rubble, as before, I made a framework of steel scaffold poles and fitted the box so that the lid comes flush with the surface of the mound, leaving an airspace all round the part which is below ground.

The entrance is again through a nine-inch-pipe tunnel, about six yards long, and I put clean straw in the box, although all bedding in the other sett has been collected by the badgers themselves.

I felt that there wasn't enough vegetation yet round the newly formed mound to give them a fair chance and that, if I didn't litter it at all, they might not be interested until more grass or reed had grown.

In order to see how long it was before they showed any interest, I bunged the mouth of the tunnel up with a gob of straw about as big as a football.

This went the first night, but it had only been a visit of curiosity for all three were in the old sett next day.

Since then, Bill has spent odd nights, at irregular intervals, in the pool sett, but I have not yet fathomed what it is that decides him. The sows have never spent a night away from the house sett, although, of course, the choice is theirs.

Because of the trouble I had when they were cubs with their eyes and skin, I handled them a great deal and they are still perfectly safe with me. But they are very shy with strangers and take immediate cover in the pipe if they smell or hear any stranger.

I have deliberately allowed them to retain as many of

their natural characteristics as possible in the hope that their behaviour will be a more reliable guide to the reactions of their wild relatives and the fact that two were reared together has influenced their attitude to Man. They are more interested in each other than they are in me.

CHAPTER EIGHT

Big Brother

The trouble with success is that it only goads ambition to further efforts. I had set out with the ambition to rear two tame badgers and see what happened when I offered them their freedom, and had finished up with three. I had wanted to find out if affections, kindled in undomesticated creatures, are as brittle and transient as ours.

Like everything else worthwhile, it had been harder to accomplish than I had thought, and I have several times regretted ever having started.

I had been tortured by conscience when it proved impossible to obtain a companion of his own age for Bill Brock, and filled with shame when I had bungled rearing the little sows next year.

Bill's affection had proved almost psychopathic and he has such a human fixation that he still prefers my company to that of his own kind. But the little sows are almost wild. They suffer me to handle them without aggressive protest, but that is the only concession to partial domesticity that they make. I wouldn't have it otherwise.

When they first come in season and Bill comes into rut, I may well have to be very much more wary how I approach even him!

I won't regret that either and I shall wish him the best of luck with his affairs.

Two years working very closely with these semi-wild badgers have taught me more than all the previous years of leisure I had been able to spend trying to find out more about their truly wild relatives.

The chief thing it has taught me is how little I still know.

The snag in my earlier badger watching had been that so much goes on when it is too dark to see. I often spent many evening hours at a sett, waiting for a badger to emerge, caught one fleeting glimpse of a white striped face in the dusk, and that was my sole reward.

Sometimes, when I got to a sett before dawn, I saw one or two return straight to the mouth of the hole, pause one instant to shake — and disappear.

The only protracted activity I could guarantee seeing was cubs at play which, beautiful as they are, is only an insignificant tithe of the potential pleasure. What goes on after dark is the real mystery.

My badgers have been reared around the house, have seen the yardlight every time I feed the dogs, and are relatively indifferent to bright illumination.

It is not, in any case, difficult to accustom badgers to artificial light, and I well remember watching a superb film, on television, which had been taken by floodlight.

The photographer had hung a low-wattage bulb above the sett, which just gave a faint glim of light. He had increased the intensity progressively, as the weeks went by, till the whole area was brilliantly lit and the badgers took no notice.

I decided to light my sett, but it wasn't much good because the times of emergence proved to be so irregular.

It is one thing to watch badgers occasionally, and to spend hours seeing nothing, and research workers have almost unlimited time.

I have a colony of badgers literally living by my window and my early success with them fired an ambition to watch them regularly, at least as much because I like badgers as for any profound scientific purpose.

Being a lazy chap at heart, I did not want to spend more time watching badgers' non-events than I could avoid, so the first thing was to establish at what periods they really were most active.

So I asked an engineer friend to rig up a contraption for me. Not a regardless-of-expense, spit-and-chromium laboratory masterpiece, but a humble bit of Heath Robinson gadgetry which, if I could afford it, would virtually have to be knocked up out of scrap.

I asked him to give me some kind of barograph which would wind a roll of graph paper past the window at constant speed.

I asked for a marking device which would 'stab' the graph, when 'told' to do so by an electric impulse. And I asked for something at the sett itself, which would make an electric contact each time a badger came or went.

My friend turned up trumps. He bought an old temperature recorder off an industrial heat treatment furnace, which is housed in a rugged, cast-iron cabinet, with a glass door, built to withstand the hurly-burly of factory life.

Not very elegant, perhaps, as a decoration for one's study, but robust enough to continue churning out records long after my head has ceased to ache.

There is an electric motor inside the cabinet, which unwinds the roll of graph paper at exactly an inch an hour.

My friend discarded the components concerned with temperature and replaced them by electro-magnets, which slam down a felt pen when the circuit is completed.

We ran a wire to the mouth of each sett and suspended a lever in a hole, cut in the top of each pipe. This lever hung through the hole, and the badgers had to swing it, like a badger gate, whenever they came in or out of the sett.

It closed an electro-micro-switch, as it swung, which activated an electro-magnet in my study and made a mark on the graph with a felt pen. Red for the house sett and black for the sett by the pool.

It was thus impossible for a badger to enter or leave either sett without the gadget in my study recording the fact as inevitably as if Big Brother himself was always watching.

There are snags, of course. The graph paper moves very slowly and the marks made by the felt pens are relatively thick. So it is possible for a badger to pass in or out several times, within a few minutes, but to leave only one distinguishable mark on the graph. Or all three may enter or leave, each closing the micro-switch correctly, but there will still only be one mark to show for it.

We did play with the idea of putting two swinging arms in each pipe, the one only operating its micro-switch when something emerged, and the other when something entered. It would then be possible in theory, to tell if the badgers were in or out, simply by examining the graph in my study.

In practice, it wouldn't be so easy because, with several badgers going in or out within a short space of time, it would need an Einstein to keep track of them.

In any case, I wanted the apparatus to help me see what they did when they came out of the sett, without having to waste time watching when nothing was happening.

So I settled for the utmost simplicity and am satisfied

with something which tells me when to look with most chance of reward without bothering too much about the niceties.

I roll the graph back each morning to the starting place of the night before, and move the pen over one of seven notches. This is duplicated on the other side of the graph, with a different coloured felt pen for the other sett.

Thus, at the end of each week, a single piece of graph paper shows a complete record of all activity at both setts for the whole week.

Simple observation, at dawn and dusk, had shown the times which the first badger left the sett and what time the last wanderer returned in the morning. But I had no idea what, if any, activity there was between times and rather assumed that they went out in the evening and didn't return till bedtime next day.

Big Brother blew that theory sky high the first week.

I found at once that there was spasmodic activity, at intervals all night, and subsequent work has shown that there appear to be fairly definite cycles of local activity, with fairly large intervals. These may be when the badgers are away foraging or when they return to the sett to rest.

It is important to realize that the long periods my badgers spend near the sett may not be true for wild badgers, because mine get a basic ration of easy food and might have to spend longer periods working for their living in the wild.

But the clues which the graph give could well form the basis for similar work on wild setts.

At some time in the future, I want to try putting pipes in the tunnels of a wild sett, and fitting micro-switches with a portable recorder, to do some confirmatory work on this and I believe that, by making alternative setts unattractive with Reynardine, it might be quite a feasible experiment.

Initial results with my two artificial setts indicate that, though there are about three periods of intense activity each night, the times are not yet predictable enough to make it profitable to watch to a timetable.

The other initial snag was that, though the graph showed what time the badgers were about, I could only see what they were doing on bright moonlight nights. And they were jolly cold in winter.

So we made a Mark II version. The only major modification was to connect two wires from the circuits which operate the electro-magnets.

These wires were taken under the study carpet, through a hole, drilled in the sitting-room wall, to a switch behind the television.

I appreciate how lucky I am to have a wife who not only tolerates such eccentricities but is actively interested in the results!

The main drive of the graph comes from the mains, but a transformer reduces the voltage to 12 for the magnets, which operate the pens, and the outside micro-switches which fit in the tunnels.

If the badgers did bite the cable through, it would not, therefore, give them a lethal shock. We, also, were able to use this twelve-volt supply under the carpet to the switch in the sitting-room, which somewhat reduces the risk of fire due to short circuits.

We wired two small twelve-volt bulbs to the switch behind the television, and one of them lights up every time a badger operates the micro-switch in the tunnel of each sett.

We are therefore warned, in the sitting-room, the

instant any activity begins, and since the warning lights sit on top of the television, we know when there is something more interesting to watch than the programme on the screen and on which sett we should concentrate.

All this, of course, would be practically useless by moonlight. So I rigged up low-power floodlights to illuminate the setts.

Although the badgers have all been brought up to be accustomed to the lights in the house and yard, an obvious criticism of the arrangement is that the fact that the sett is externally lit might influence the times of emergence, so we had to modify it once more.

We put the floodlighting in circuit so that it does not come on until a badger comes along the tunnel. Until he actually emerges, there is only natural light – or darkness. So the artificial light cannot have influenced his initial movements.

When he trips the micro-switch, but not before, the graph is marked, the setts are floodlit and we are warned by the pilot lights on the television. All simultaneously.

It is easy to show that, in practice, artificial light has little effect. I leave the floodlight disconnected one night each week, but the patterns on the graph are apparently unaffected and it is impossible to tell, by subsequent inspection, which night there was no light.

The electro-magnets, which operate the felt pens, have about an inch of travel and go with a sufficient bang to be audible in the bedroom, above, in the still of the night.

So, although we did not connect warning lights upstairs, we know when there is activity because we can hear the graph being thumped.

It is often possible to pop out of bed to watch whatever is going on, though I plan to rig up a series of mirrors, so that I can lie in bed and watch in comfort.

The first result that surprised me was the amount of time spent at and around the sett itself.

Seeing it on the graph, before I connected the flood-light, I imagined most of it was ritual bed-making.

In daylight, I had seen them scratch herbage until it is lacerated enough to tear free, when they tucked away a tangled ball of grass under their chins and backed away up the pipe, as Bill had done the first day I'd introduced him to the sett.

This method of collection was so thorough that the steep side of the bank nearest the sett appears perman-ently mown, and there are often wisps of grass at the mouth of the tunnel in the morning.

The obvious conclusion was that such tedious work must take a long time, and that it was probably this which accounted for a great deal of the marks which appeared on the graph each morning.

It turned out that they fritter away much of their time on far less productive work than this. Indeed, their activity could scarcely be described more accurately than 'messing about.'

The old boar is almost always first out. The warning light indicates that, within a few seconds, he will be in view.

Turning from the television, we see his black and white face, framed for a few seconds, in the mouth of the tunnel, while his sensitive nose tests the breeze for friends or foes.

Then he comes out, climbs the mound and over the other side, to empty himself in his latrine, right on the boundary fence.

This marking of the edge of his territory seems quite as important to him as his physical comfort.

Sometimes the two sows follow at intervals of a minute

or less, but at others there is no sign of them at all.

The first to show up always tests the breeze, as Bill has done, but her next move is usually to sharpen her claws on the tree root which covers the pipe entrance.

'Sharpen' may well be the wrong word, because badgers' claws are not sharp, since they get blunted by digging and are not retractable or designed for holding their prey.

She scratches the root, about a foot above the ground, as a cat will stand up against an upholstered chair and shred the cover. Perhaps the purpose is to clean the claws of any particles of soil, from last night's digging, or to shell off any overgrown or damaged pieces of nail.

The sows have a whole series of very small latrines within a radius of three or four yards of the mouth of the sett.

They often urinate in these and then go straight back to bed, seeming far less preoccupied with territory marking than the boar, and only go to the larger latrine pits, further off, for complete evacuation.

At odd times, Bill decides to sleep away in the pool sett. It is not yet clear what influences this, as he will sometimes go weeks without sleeping there and then, for no apparent reason, he will stay for three or four consecutive days.

I have tried relating this to temperature and weather conditions, but have not yet stumbled on the controlling factor.

Even when he is at the pool sett, he is always the first up and about. The pool light flashes, he tests the breeze and goes down to the pool to drink. Then he usually goes round the edge of the paddock, just inside the wood, and emerges opposite my study window.

He tests that, to see if I am about, and, if he draws

blank, he goes round the edge of the ha-ha to the house sett.

Here he stops, with his head inside the tunnel, and within a few moments one or both of the sows is out.

I believe he calls, probably with the affectionate whinny he gives on seeing me, but that is another of the things I shall enjoy finding out.

I intend to wire the sett for a microphone, as well as for light, so that I can make a series of recordings of badger language, to evaluate against the actions I can observe.

The first young sow to come to the mouth of the sett, pauses, as usual, to test the breeze. Bill has no patience with this.

He knows all is well, because he has been out and about while these young layabouts have been lazing deep in slumber.

So he grabs the young sow by the scruff of her neck and drags her unceremoniously out. He holds her as a hob ferret holds his jill, when he is about to mate her, and I believe that this is the initial sex play which grows more and more pronounced as the year creeps on towards the rut.

The sow makes no protest, but allows him to drag her passively about for perhaps ten or fifteen seconds.

Then he lets her go and turns his back on her.

He raises his tail vertically and backs rapidly towards her. She stands her ground and allows him to make forcible contact and taint her with his musk.

I confirmed this by going out immediately and picking the young sow up and discovered that she reeked of musk as strong as if she had been frightened and tainted herself.

I have not yet been able to discover if it is always the

same sow which comes out first, perhaps indicating monogamy, or if it is just a matter of chance which is honoured by his demonstrative caress.

The two sows are so alike that I cannot tell them apart, though they were very different in size when they came, and reputed to be from widely separate colonies, and therefore unrelated.

This will help, so far as providing fresh blood is concerned, if they prove co-operative enough to raise families, but it is no help for specific observation.

I have mulled around in my mind what I can do to distinguish them. I detest toe-clipping, which is widely practised amongst scientific mammalogists for identification, because it is nothing but a polite name for painful mutilation. In any case, it would not help to distinguish them at a distance.

There is never any confusion between the boar and the sows, because the boar is considerably bigger and the shape of his head is quite different. Much longer and stronger, so that the sows' heads seem wedge-shaped, by comparison.

They really are as alike as two peas and, for any short-term experiments, I suppose I could put a dab of sheep dye on one of them or clip a patch of fur, to expose her lighter undercoat.

Do not assume from this that I am a desiccated academic dedicated to the search of pure knowledge, for its own sake and at whatever expense. I am merely interested in badgers because I like them and want to know as much about them as possible so that I can enjoy them better; so that I can exploit the knowledge, by taking short cuts to observing them, using a higher proportion of my time watching something happen instead of waiting for nothing to happen.

Most important of all, I want to amass facts to build up a viable case for their preservation and to be able to out-argue, from factual experience, those who would do them harm on hearsay evidence.

Some of the facts, which I have already observed, I think will help. There is now no doubt whatever in my mind that their depredations amongst game have been vastly overrated, as experiments with my duck and pheasants have shown.

On the other hand, I have no doubt that, if a domestic hen is stupid enough to remain on the ground at night, and fails to take evasive action because she runs into the wire netting or thick cover, then her doom is sealed.

So if, as sometimes happens, a poultry keeper rings up to say that a badger has opened the shutter in his hen pen, entered and killed the poultry, and is then unable to escape, I never plead for clemency.

My advice is to shoot him in the midst of his guilt because otherwise, I fear, he will become a persistent offender and get all badgers an undeserved bad name. There is nothing more damaging to any cause than pleading black is white in the face of objective evidence to the contrary.

My experiments in containing badgers have also proved rewarding. The perimeter netting round my enclosure has a narrow plinth of concrete along one side. A taut strand of barbed wire is pegged to this through holes left when the concrete was laid, and the netting is laced to the barbed wire.

This is extremely effective and no badger has ever broached it because they always start digging at the bottom of the netting and the concrete defeats them.

It does not occur to them to dig six inches away from the base, where it would be simple for such a powerful digger to tunnel under the concrete.

The snag in this method is that a shallow trench has to be dug by hand and that the concrete is relatively expensive.

Wherever else we could, we ploughed a furrow, put the netting and barbed wire in the bottom of the trench and turned the furrow back by hand.

This is all right, provided the returned soil consolidates properly, but badgers work always at the boundary, ever probing for weakness, and if the netting does not feel solid, they unfailingly dig.

They dig latrine pits along the boundary, too, to mark it as territory, and if they come across a piece of soft ground they go on digging.

In the wood itself, we had to dig the netting in by hand and often encountered immovable roots. The netting is naturally shallow each side of these and therefore vulnerable.

This would not keep a determined badger in or out, as we proved when the wild boar, which got into the paddock to fight Bill, had escaped from the enclosure by morning.

It seems to me that my enclosure of about six acres of very varied terrain is probably about the minimum that badgers would accept without constantly trying for more.

Normally, ours have the freedom of the woods, outside, because I now believe that strange badgers are unlikely to attack them until the strangers are *established* in a sett which includes our area within its traditional territory.

So I examine my neighbour's sett regularly and stink it out the moment a hole is opened up, and I patrol the boundary fence for signs of territory-marking latrine pits on the outside.

At the first sign of danger, I fasten our badgers in till

I have driven the interlopers off.

My reason for believing our enclosure more or less adequate for them is that they make no herculean efforts to escape, even when they have been used to the unlimited freedom of the wood outside.

They seem perfectly content, though they eat more of the artificial food I put.

Without supplementary feeding, the area they require would doubtless be greater except in seasons of exceptional plenty.

When badgers really do mean business, they take a deal of stopping, especially from areas they consider theirs by right.

When I discovered that a channel of water was no deterrent to mine going round the back of the pool, I experimented with ordinary agricultural electric fence, designed to keep cattle where they are wanted. I erected a length, six inches high, within a foot of my study window, where I could observe it.

Bill calls there, every night of his life, and is beginning to mark the metal window frame, and even the glass, with pieces of flint, which become imbedded in the horn of his claws when he is digging.

The live electric wire was so close to the window that he couldn't avoid making firm contact, the whole time he was scratching to get in.

These agricultural electric fences give a high voltage shock, similar to a car's sparking plug, but the current they carry is not dangerous.

I switched on, when he was due to visit me and, feeling rather mean, I settled down to watch.

It might as well not have been there. He ambled up, with his great, leathery pads flat on the wet stone step, making, I thought, the perfect contact to earth.

Seeing something strange, he put his wet nose directly on the bare wire and I was horrified lest I had overdone it, and it might do him harm. But he never even noticed it.

Without so much as flinching, he lumbered over it, sat on it and started to scrape at the window.

The same electric wire round a fowl pen or pheasant run would have been more than enough to send all the foxes which touched it, non stop into the next parish.

Most of the sheer mischief in badgers' breasts seems to have been dissipated by the time they are adults, and the sows were never as provocative as Bill, perhaps because they work off their surplus energy on each other.

When Bill was a cub, he took sadistic delight in grabbing the turn-ups of my trousers and shaking them till they tore or until I capitulated and picked him up. And Stanley Porter, who has taken the pictures in this book, found to his cost that a photographic hide, placed anywhere within reach, would not hide much next day.

Even though such heartiness wears off with maturity, I was worried about the fate of the duck, especially the pinioned duck, in time of deep snow.

We had a fairly heavy fall in February '69 and the ducks kept a free hole on the pool, as a retreat, so for a couple of weeks there were no casualties.

Then I noticed a patch of blood, on the snow, by the wood, and, on inspection, there were unmistakable badger tracks all round. In the centre, were the remains of a carolina duck.

This would have been evidence enough for execution, had most keepers found it, and it was only by coincidence that I knew the truth.

The day before, a movement in the paddock caught my eye, as I was writing at my desk, and, looking up, I saw two carrion crows mobbing a carolina duck.

She was an old duck, which had never been a good specimen, and I had noticed lately that she seemed to be getting even more decrepit. So much so that I had been tempted to destroy her lest she transmit some disease to the others.

The crows had obviously sensed a weakling, and were dive bombing her when I stopped writing to watch.

The duck had panicked and the crows had cut her off from the pool and were driving her into deepening snow. It was a technique I'd seen crows adopt with young rabbits and leverets, but never with anything so large as a duck.

One attracted her attention, while the other buffeted her from behind, each attack making her fluster farther away from safety.

I was intrigued to know if their attack would be fatal so, instead of going straight for my ·22 rifle, I watched a while.

It soon became evident that, if nothing was done, they would finish her off, so I went for the rifle, intending to have a shot at one crow and then to go and put the duck out of her misery, too.

When I returned, neither crows nor duck were anywhere to be seen, so I assumed that she had made a supreme effort and regained the sanctuary of water.

It turned out that I was wrong and that she had sunk in a snowdrift, for I found her remains surrounded by badger tracks next morning.

I imagine that the badgers, on their rounds, got scent of her, retrieved her from the snow and had a tasty snack.

It would have needed no skilled QC to have obtained a conviction but the evidence was misleading and the badgers were not to blame.

It has surprised me how much they are abroad, not only in frosty weather, but in snow too.

I knew, of course, that they come out in snow, because I had seen their tracks, but it never occurred to me that it would be for more than the minimum time required to empty themselves and take on more food.

The barograph in my study told a story which dispelled such illusions. It showed that they were out and about almost as much as usual.

Bill, as usual, breaks the ice first. He goes through the normal routine and then he comes towards the house, almost out of sight, along the ha-ha slope.

It is quite obvious that he is enjoying himself. He cavorts about and is soon followed by the sows.

By morning, there is no doubt where they have been, and their tracks are trenched through the deep snow, almost like the play slides made by otters.

I always take the opportunity of snow to walk, not only the whole of our boundaries, but those of my neighbours, too. I can then make certain where the nearest colony of wild badgers is working and where they cross on to our land.

I can see the fox runs, too, so that, if they trouble me later on, I know where to set a wire.

I am always careful to avoid the modern 'self-lock' wires which are diabolical, unselective killers of dogs or badgers or any other creature which is unlucky enough to become entangled. With the old-fashioned ones, the badgers have usually broken free by next day, or, at worst, are waiting to be cut free when I arrive next morning.

I mark out a plan, from the evidence of the snow, and put a barrowful of sand at strategic places, when it has thawed, so that I can see, all the following summer, what is about, almost as well as if it had just snowed.

Evidence from the barograph needs careful translation. It shows, for example, that both our setts are visited almost every night. They often spend most of their spare time at the pool sett in hours of darkness, though they go to the house sett at dawn.

It a keeper noticed recent work at a sett, put a terrier through and found nothing there, he would say that it had been recently used, but that the badgers had moved to another sett. It could well have been the foundation on which stories of badgers leaving a sett when it is stale are based.

I know that the evidence of my badgers is suspect, because I cannot claim them to be truly wild. But at least their activities can point the way for future investigations to confirm or confound the results by watching wild colonies. At least, they may help us to know what to look for.

Meanwhile, they live a slightly precarious existence, dependent, in part, on my ability to protect them from attack by wild badgers. It is an absorbing example of conservation by constructive wild-life management.

I have the advantages of co-operative neighbours, of ninety acres of territory which is eminently suitable for badgers, and a sizeable enclosure, where I can confine them in times of danger.

Yet I still walk the knife edge which only makes it practicable to live with badgers as I do, and I examine my graph every morning, with bated breath, to check that all is well.

The experiment is successful so far and my badgers are leading full and happy lives. Long may they continue their nightly calls at my window!

Footnote

Since writing the above, one of the sows failed to return and it has been impossible to establish what happened to her.

Some clue was provided within a week or so when a local visitor asked how 'our' badgers were getting on. When I told him that one had disappeared but that the old boar and remaining sow were all right, he expressed surprise.

'You're lucky to have any left,' he said, 'because we've wired five, in the last few weeks, in fox-hangs, and they all seemed to come from your direction. I didn't think you'd have any left.'

Although he is not an immediate neighbour, he lives well within the territory that our badgers might be expected to explore, and my instinctive impulse was to do him violence.

Concealing my feelings as best I could, I asked what damage badgers did to him.

'They are as big as dogs,' he said, 'so they are bound to eat a lot. And, since they have teeth like a dog, they are bound to do some damage.' But he did not say what the damage was.

I pointed to our wild duck, feeding fearlessly within a few yards of our setts, and suggested that we had more than he had.

'Yes,' he said, 'I've just counted over thirty and some pheasants, too. All I can say is that you must be very lucky.'

He was quite impervious to reasoned argument in the badgers' favour, and obviously regarded me as anti-social for harbouring such 'vermin'.

So I asked him to co-operate by refraining from using self-lock snares.

I check that my badgers are safely home every morning and would have some chance of finding one caught in a conventional free-running snare and releasing it before it died of strangulation.

But the first struggles in a self-lock snare often do such damage that eventual death is inevitable.

Legal protection would not be an effectual answer since it simply would not work on secluded private property unless the owner was convinced that the law was sensible.

It will take years of education to erode the traditional fallacies that everything with a hooked bill or canine teeth should be exterminated to avoid the chance that the odd pheasant should die from any cause but gunshot.

So far as my project here is concerned, it is now several months since we had any trouble from aggression by wild badgers and it seems that our badgers have at last established their territory.

If local people will co-operate by giving them a chance, perhaps they will learn from experience how little harm they do.

P.D.

Index

Foot and mouth disease, 91, 92
Forestry Commission policy with badgers, 18
Fox hunters kill badger, 26
Fox hunting and badger digging, 26-7
Frog as quarry, 89, 90

Gamekeepers and predators, 20-1
Gassing badgers, 21, 24, 27, 28
Gatecrashing a party, 86-7
Gripton the terrier man, 33, 34
Grooming by dogs, 72, 73

Handrearing cubs, 36-43, 68, 69
Harmless badgers, 99

Incentives in training, 73, 74
Increasing badger population, 22
Injuries from fighting, 102, 109, 110
Introducing strange badgers, 127-9
Introduction to dogs. 71, 72
Introduction to strange setts, 63-6, 81-2, 132

Latrine in sett. 101
Latrine pits, 84
Learning territory, 76, 90, 128
Learning to hunt, 131
Liberating tame badgers, 117
Light warns of activity, 143-4
Limiting gassing to professional pest officers, 27-8
Loss of appetite, 48

Malpractices of badger digs, 20
Marking territory, 118

Memory for territory, 104

Nature Conservancy licence to destroy, 25

Otter hunting, 17

Persecution, 14
Pet cubs, 14-15
Photographing badgers, 32, 152
Pine marten, 20
Play, 128, 130
Play with dogs, 39-40
Preservation of mammals, 22
Preservation of badgers, 149
Preserving pheasants from foxes, by badgers, 94
Press photographers, 45
Protection of otters, 17

Rat held by tail, 111
Reaction to water, 134
Recording vocabulary, 147
Releasing, 16
Removing badgers from artificial fox earths, 67, 68
Rescue dig, 57-9
Rogue badgers, 28

Setts dangerous to farm machinery, 23-4
Sex play 147
Sharpening claws on emergence, 146
Sitting birds, 95-6
Snaring badgers, 22
Snaring foxes, 154
Sow cubs, 107-8
'Spotting' musk, 41
Suggested legislation for control, 22, 23
Swimming, 134